T0243200

COMPETITIVE
SUCCESS

ARJAN SINGH

COMPETITIVE
SUCCESS

Building Winning Strategies with
CORPORATE WAR GAMES

Forbes | Books

Published by Forbes Books, Charleston, South Carolina.
An imprint of Advantage Media Group.

Forbes Books is a registered trademark, and the Forbes Books colophon is a trademark of Forbes Media, LLC.

Printed in the United States of America.

10 9 8 7 6 5 4 3 2 1

ISBN: 979-8-88750-324-0 (Hardcover)
ISBN: 979-8-88750-325-7 (eBook)

Library of Congress Control Number: 2023921803

Cover design by Megan Elger.
Layout design by Analisa Smith.

This custom publication is intended to provide accurate information and the opinions of the author in regard to the subject matter covered. It is sold with the understanding that the publisher, Forbes Books, is not engaged in rendering legal, financial, or professional services of any kind. If legal advice or other expert assistance is required, the reader is advised to seek the services of a competent professional.

Since 1917, Forbes has remained steadfast in its mission to serve as the defining voice of entrepreneurial capitalism. Forbes Books, launched in 2016 through a partnership with Advantage Media, furthers that aim by helping business and thought leaders bring their stories, passion, and knowledge to the forefront in custom books. Opinions expressed by Forbes Books authors are their own. To be considered for publication, please visit **books.Forbes.com**.

This book is dedicated to my family, who provided unwavering support, love and understanding to help bring this book to life. Your encouragement and belief have been the foundation upon which this book stands.

To my wife, who has believed in me through every stage of my career, I extend my deepest gratitude.

To my children, who provided endless love and understanding, I am grateful beyond words.

To my parents and brother, whose belief in my abilities go back to the very beginning, your guidance and unwavering support throughout my life have shaped me into the person I am today.

CONTENTS

ACKNOWLEDGMENTS xi

INTRODUCTION 1

CHAPTER 1 17
WHAT IS A WAR GAME?

CHAPTER 2 29
BUILDING WINNING STRATEGIES

CHAPTER 3 39
CORE ATTRIBUTES FOR COMPETITIVE SUCCESS

CHAPTER 4 53
HOW IS WAR GAMING BETTER THAN TRADITIONAL PLANNING?

CHAPTER 5 67
HOW DO I GET STARTED?

CHAPTER 6 73
IDENTIFYING YOUR WAR GAME OBJECTIVES

CHAPTER 7 83

ASSESSING THE FIELD OF BATTLE

CHAPTER 8 95

UNDERSTANDING THE KEY COMPETITORS

CHAPTER 9 103

ANALYZING PREVIOUS BATTLES

CHAPTER 10 117

GATHERING INTELLIGENCE

CHAPTER 11 133

ASSESSING TROOP STRENGTH, MORALE, AND RESOURCES

CHAPTER 12 153

DECIDING ON SCENARIOS AND TACTICS

CHAPTER 13 171

CONDUCTING THE WAR GAME

CHAPTER 14 189

MOVING FROM WAR ROOM TO REAL WORLD

CONCLUSION 197

APPENDIX 201

ACKNOWLEDGMENTS

B ehind every author's success are mentors and guides whose unwavering belief in them paves the way. I have been exceptionally fortunate to have received invaluable guidance and inspiration from a cadre of remarkable individuals throughout my career.

I extend my profound gratitude to Michael Sandman, whose introduction to the world of war games and our globe-trotting war game adventures set me on an extraordinary path. I am deeply thankful to Leonard Fuld for shaping my early understanding of Competitive Intelligence, Dr. Leonard Lane for igniting my passion for teaching at the graduate level, and to Bill Dillon and David Jacobson for their unwavering support in realizing my vision of creating distinctive learning experiences for students at the SMU Cox School of Business.

Lastly, my heartfelt thanks go out to all those who generously shared their knowledge and expertise over the years—it is your collective influence that has breathed life into this book.

INTRODUCTION

A good hockey player plays where the puck is. A great hockey player plays where the puck is going to be.

—WAYNE GRETZKY

In 2006, I started co-teaching a competitive intelligence course that I designed for the University of California, Irvine's (UCI) School of Business. The final exam was eight hours long. To this day, it holds the record for the longest final exam in the UC system. Of course, the students balked after reading through the syllabus on the first day of class. "*What?*" They collectively exclaimed, "You're putting us through an eight-hour final exam? Are you *crazy?*"

The final exam wasn't a grueling paper or tortuous multiple-choice test. It was a *war game*; the same kind of war game that the military has been using to plan battles for thousands of years. At the end of that first class, the feedback was the following: "Wow! This was amazing! What a great experience! We wish we had more time." Word got out quickly, and after that first semester, each new class immediately filled up on the first day of registration.

Obviously, in business the battlefield isn't along a front and the stakes aren't life or death, as it is in war. The battlefield in my war game is the competitive marketplace and the stakes are *winning*. Money, power, and fame are certainly drivers, but a large part of success is the feeling of satisfaction and self-confidence that results from beating the competition and coming out on top.

To win, the students needed to learn what the game was, and how to play the game—to identify and study their adversaries, to assess their company's strengths and weaknesses, to brainstorm battle scenarios, and to test various offensives. In business, war gaming isn't paranoia; it's about being smart, shrewd, and controlling your destiny so you can succeed. This is why war games are the perfect tool for business students, leaders of corporations, and even individuals.

One of the first war game finals I held for my class at UCI was the "Battle for Home Entertainment." We had several media and entertainment industry teams such as Fox, Microsoft, Verizon, and Apple. The students didn't know which company they were going to represent until they pulled the company name out of a hat at the start of the final. Their first task was to read the Briefing Book, as a team, for the companies they represented, which contained market and company overviews.

The second exercise was for each team to build a base case strategy for their companies. For the final exercise, I would run them all through a stress test, or a "scenario." The question was what if this scenario happens in the world? What would you do, and how would this effect or change your base strategy? (This war game final is an abbreviated version of what happens in a corporate war game, where I run leaders through a minimum of four to five rounds of competitive exercises.) For the Battle for Home Entertainment, the key question

I gave the students was the following: Who's going to control the living room?

After a few hours, the Apple team came back and said, "Look, we've done an analysis of our company, and we've literally got nothing in the living room. We've got Macs that people use for productivity. And we've got iPods for music." (I know what you're thinking, but remember that in 2006, iPads hadn't yet been invented.) I told them to keep pushing.

After a few more rounds, they picked up a small empty random box and said, "OK, today we announce what we call iTV. This is a box that allows you to view streaming content on your TV."

They won. And here's why: That was December 2006. In March 2007, three months later, Apple introduced the world for the first time to Apple TV.

I gave a group of business students a toolkit in the form of a war-gaming process, which included a Briefing Book and a simple scenario. And with that, in eight hours they came up with a winning strategy; the same real-world strategy which Apple announced three months later.

Fast-forward to May 27, 2017, where I ran a war game final called "Battle for the Traveler" again at UC Irvine. It involved six different companies from the travel industry: Delta, Booking.com, Expedia, TripAdvisor, Marriott, and Airbnb. The scenario was the following: What would happen if some external black-swan event caused a sudden 95 percent decline in the US domestic travel market, similar to 9/11?

At that time, the strategy for every US travel company was based upon a single core assumption: continued expansion. As a response, they were trying to control travelers by incentivizing the cheapest, most convenient options, e.g., "Book on our website and we'll give you_____."

The students were skeptical. They argued, "No way this is ever going to happen again! This is a stupid scenario!" But I told them that's precisely the point of war gaming. You prepare for the worst and then hope for the best. You strategize for the future based on the greatest impact to your business, not probability.

And, ironically, the exercise turned out to be predictive of the COVID-19 pandemic.

I sometimes ideate negative scenarios for war gaming that challenge assumptions companies make about their industries. I ask questions such as the following: "What if there isn't a recovery this year? What if it's slower than it's what it's supposed to be?" The lesson not only that my students learned in Battle for the Traveler, but that the global economy learned from COVID-19, is the fallibility of a solely linear strategy.

In other words, if we're in the year 2023, we strategize until 2028, usually two, five, or ten years at most. The world, we assume, is going to continue the way it's going. COVID-19 taught us that we can and likely will experience massive disruptions. War gaming is both a reactive and predictive way to look at the world, and that's extremely valuable if you want to win. When you put a team of talented, smart people into a relaxed, low risk, competitive atmosphere, you create a safe space for innovation.

HOW I GOT INTO WAR GAMING

Getting into war gaming was a path that came easily to me, thanks to my family, who, since I can remember, have always been involved in international politics. My grandfather, Sardar Swaran Singh, served as a cabinet minister of India for twenty-four years and worked as a close advisor for Prime Minister Jawaharlal Nehru. He still holds the record for the longest continuously serving cabinet member in India's history. My father and uncle were senior government officials dealing with strategic and intelligence matters. At the dinner table, we'd talk Cold War politics, speculating about the USSR and its pullout from Afghanistan and discussing geopolitics in China. When I was ten years old, I read magazines such as the *Far Eastern Economic Review* and *BusinessWeek*. This all was like a master class on higher-level strategic thinking.

These lessons from my childhood came in handy when I went to university in Switzerland. I was taking a marketing class, and we were doing a case study around Southwest Airlines' strategy. My roommate and I were more interested in playing PlayStation than the class. One day while were playing we realized we were, once again, late. We literally did the homework running to class.

When the teacher asked, "Who knows this break-even point for Southwest?" I kept quiet, but my friend nudged me.

I whispered, "No, I don't know if it's right or not and he's scary. I don't want to be the focus of his attention."

The teacher saw and asked, "Do you have something to say?"

I put my number on the board and he said, "Yeah, that's the right answer." I was the only one who gave the correct answer. But it wasn't because I spent hours and hours doing it. The teacher was surprised.

A few students in the class worked for a competitive intelligence consultancy. They asked me, "Hey, do you want to work on some projects with us?"

I said, "No, I've got all these other things I'm doing."

They came back a week later and asked again. The project was doing research to map out the competitive global supply chain for a pharmaceutical product in the US about to go generic. I agreed to help and that project went really well, so I worked on a few more projects until they recruited me to run a whole practice in Europe by the time I graduated.

Early on in my career I started asking myself, "Are there other ways to do this that might make a bigger impact for my clients?" I wanted my clients to make decisions based on data versus guessing. At the time, I was teaching a class on competitive intelligence and in parallel, a colleague was teaching a class on war gaming for corporate strategy. I saw that in war gaming, you build decisions based on data; you have a direct line on what's going on. This is very different from a traditional consultancy. Usually, if you hire a consultancy they'll tell you, "Here's what the answers are and we're the smartest people in the room, so you should believe it."

What really got me into war gaming was observing my students. It made me think that if a company can build strategies on data *and* get experience, then they can accelerate their learning. I prefer having people in a company use a toolkit of proven techniques that work for them to come up with their own outputs, just like my students. And now, after running over 200 war games, I believe this methodology is fundamental to any company's success.

What I tell my clients is that in a complex global and competitive world, formulating a plan without testing it is the equivalent of walking into a battlefield without the right weapons or a plan to win. War gaming helps companies understand and defend against external threats. It answers questions such as the following:

- How is the marketplace changing?

- Where and what are our competitors investing in?

- How is the competition targeting us?

- How are our competitors preparing for these anticipated changes?

It's not uncommon for organizations to be too inwardly focused when developing their strategies and tactics. This isn't sustainable in the long term. War gaming is a powerful, effective tool for dealing with situations when a strategy might not work. And the only way you can find that out yourself is by testing it.

In over twenty-five years as a consultant, I've discovered that it's easy to deliver good news, because when it's good news, everyone loves you. I had a Chief Financial Officer run with my good news. Even though it was untested, he didn't care. The result was a $200 million upside to the business.

But, when I give bad news like, "Your strategy's not going to work. You're not going to meet your targets and your stock will suffer," I'm essentially calling their baby ugly.

Naturally, they respond: "You don't know what you're talking about," or find a multitude of reasons to justify in their minds why the bad news is flawed.

If someone disagrees, I tell them, "If you disagree, you might know something that I don't, in which case please tell me why and I'll change. I'll add to the evidence, I'll add to the assumptions, and I'll change my conclusion. Or maybe I've told you a hard truth that you didn't know, and you don't want to receive it?"

Now the conversation evolves from "You don't know what you're talking about," to "Let's have an honest conversation internally and walk through this in a safe environment." This puts us in a prime position for war gaming. It's a safe internal environment where we can challenge, test, and formulate assumptions before finding out the hard way in the marketplace.

And nobody wants to find out the hard way.

A transparent framework is critical for developing actionable intelligence:

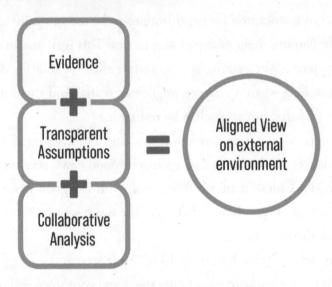

UNTESTED STRATEGIES (AKA UGLY BABIES)

Some companies might have a strategy, but it hasn't been tested. I'm sure you've read about how Blockbuster had a meeting with Netflix where Blockbuster basically told Netflix their baby was ugly. Blockbuster argued their assumption that people want to come into a store to physically browse movies and then choose one and go home. Netflix argued that no, people don't want to do that. They want the movies to come to their mailbox within a day or two. Then they offered to sell themselves for $50 million to Blockbuster, and Blockbuster laughed them out of the room. Netflix is now a $150 billion company, and Blockbuster's gone from a few thousand stores across the US to one.

Yahoo was offered a chance to buy Google for only $1 million in 1997. At the time, Google was a fledgling startup run out of a garage, but the founders, Sergey Brin and Larry Page, had invented an algorithm for search. Yahoo was buying plenty of other Silicon Valley startups, like another search engine company called Net Controls for $1.4 million. Even so, they passed on the deal of a lifetime because they wanted to keep people on the Yahoo homepage, which was loaded down with banner ads.[1]

The same thing happened to MySpace. In 2005, Mark Zuckerberg offered to sell Facebook to MySpace for $75 million. MySpace turned him down. A few months later, Zuckerberg came back and said they could buy Facebook for $750 million—the entire company! Again, they said no. MySpace was acquired by News Corp for $580 million in 2006. In the fall of 2007, Microsoft bought 1.6 percent of Facebook for $240 million—at a $15 billion valuation! That same year the co-owners of MySpace negotiated a scant $50 million, two-year contract with News Corp. Facebook by that time was earning twice the traffic.

FAILURE TO EXECUTE (NEGLECTED BABIES)

Some companies have tested their strategies, but they can't execute. Kodak had the intellectual property for digital photography and the technology, but they misinterpreted the market and assumed digital to be an *expansion* of their core business, rather than an *entirely new* business. Ultimately, they bet on analog continuing and it cost them.

Toys"R"Us made the same mistake. They also saw the disruption in the market, but they bet on specialty retailing as their core business and e-commerce as an enhancement. They were slowly choked from the early 2000s on by e-commerce giant Amazon and big box stores like Target and Walmart, who bet on lowest price and convenience. Toys"R"Us filed for bankruptcy in 2017 and in 2018, closing all of their retail stores and selling their intellectual property rights to WGN.

---

1   Krisztian Bocsi, "As Yahoo sunsets, a 22-year timeline of its 12 biggest mistakes," n.d., Bizwomen.com.

WAR GAMING FOR COMPETITIVE SUCCESS

War gaming isn't a new concept. I had a Southern Methodist University (SMU) student who went through my course and said, "This is exactly what we were taught in the military. We went through a war-gaming exercise!" While the basic process is similar to traditional, military war gaming, my modern way of war gaming is adapted for this world, a world in which we are constantly experiencing dynamic changes. We have less time to react because of technology, and we must make crucial decisions in real time. Our world is increasingly more virtual, as well. I've adapted the war-gaming methodology for virtual, interactive modalities.

In traditional war gaming, you go through an intellectual exercise and at the end of it you're likely to ask, "What do I do with this now?" A lot of companies in the past have gone through war games, gotten some great insights, and then went right back to work, ignoring the outputs. Effective war gaming is about *doing*, not just *thinking about doing*. The difference between an *interesting* workshop and an *actionable* workshop is developing a competitive success Playbook and using it. My approach has evolved into a practical integration into business that makes an impact. It's not just the war game itself, but the process beforehand and the follow-up afterward.

YOUR COMPETITIVE SUCCESS PLAYBOOK

I was working with a global consumer products company whose product, sold in 200 countries, was being subjected to increasingly extreme and complex regulations. We started with a pilot in a few different countries, among them Kazakhstan, Korea, Australia, and Greece, and then they took that methodology and rolled it out for the rest of the countries. We also war gamed the possibility that one or more of their products might not be approved. In fact, one of their products was not approved, but we had a Playbook in place for that. Their product did eventually get approval and earned the company $1 billion in 2022.

My hope for you with this book is that you can test pilot your own war game, creating a process that is scalable and applicable to all levels of your business. This book will be your competitive Playbook, where you build your strategy before things happen, stress test it, integrate your tested strategy into a business plan, and finally make sure you execute on it afterward.

War gaming is effective on all three levels of analysis:

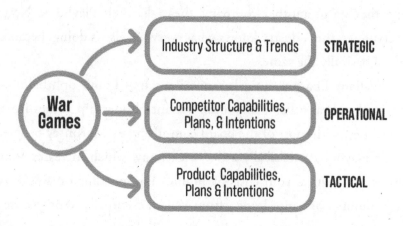

1. Strategic (industry structure and trends): What's the industry going to look like in five years? What do you need to have in place to be able to compete in the future?

2. Operational (competitor capabilities, plans, and intentions): How do you define the game that you're in? In other words, where do you want to play? Are you a manufacturer? Are you a service provider?

3. Tactical (product capabilities, plans, and intentions): How do you win? What capabilities do you need to have in place to execute for the win?

SCENARIOS AND YOUR COMPETITIVE SUCCESS PLAYBOOK

With traditional strategic planning, most companies have a defined process to build their strategies and execution plan, but it has its limitations, as it's mainly an inside-out approach. Johnson & Johnson runs a Marketing Excellence Academy designed to teach their executive leadership the basic Playbook. All leadership goes through this mandatory training. The problem is, when these leaders leave and they go to another company, they take their Playbook. Now, everyone in the industry knows what everyone else is doing, because it's all basically the same.

Valiant Pharmaceuticals owns Bausch + Lomb ophthalmology and several other companies. Valiant's leadership comes from McKinsey, with most of the board comprising ex-McKinsey people. Their Playbook is basically a one-trick pony, which increases your prices and reduces your costs by minimizing spending on R&D. A large number of senior leaders from Valiant eventually went to other pharmaceutical companies, taking their Playbook with them. Guess what happened? Now we have an entire industry all using the same Playbook.

With war gaming, you layer on scenarios to keep your Playbook fresh and relevant in a constantly changing world. Instead of thinking from the inside-out, you think as your competition, from the outside-in. If you're looking at a public competitor, there's certain guidance that they give with huge assumptions underlying their plan. You can tie a war game to your competition's guidance by using their own Playbook. This is very powerful as it keeps your Playbook fresh.

I ran a war game for a company in the industrial maintenance, repair, and operations (MRO) space. Their largest competitor was being very aggressive in the marketplace. But I knew their leadership and was familiar with how much they relied on him and his Playbook. One of the scenarios I ran was the following: What if your competitor, Home Depot, loses interest in the business? And they responded, "You're crazy. They're not going to lose interest in the business!" I argued, "What if the CEO disappears?" One year later, the CEO did leave and Home Depot divested HD Supply for $8.5 billion, creating a huge opportunity for my client to immediately step in with their tested strategy.[2] They were prepared for this situation, as they war gamed it, and it did not come as a surprise.

WAR GAMING AND OVERCOMING RESISTANCE FROM WITHIN

Let's talk about that ugly baby again. Whether it's good news or bad news, any kind of change usually meets with resistance. War gaming is a way to show leadership the problem, by walking them through it and allowing them to reach their own conclusions, rather than just telling them. This gets buy-in and ownership.

I ran a game recently for a pharmaceutical product, which was a combination of two different products in one pill. One scenario I proposed was the following: What if your customer just buys two separate pills and takes them rather than your one pill? And at first, leadership responded, "Well, that's not going to happen." So, I opened it up to the thirty participants from their own leadership team and

---

2   "Home Depot to buy back HD Supply in $8 billion deal" The Home Depot, November 16, 2020, https://www.cnbc.com/2020/11/16/home-depot-to-buy-hd-supply-hold-ings-in-an-8-billion-deal.html.

asked them, "What would be the most disruptive event in your marketplace?"

Everyone took a Post-it and wrote what they thought, putting it on the wall. Then I gave them all two stickers, one for each vote and asked them to vote on the two events they thought would be the most impactful to their marketplace. And within two minutes, we had prioritization in the form of the top ten scenarios. We only had time for three, so we tackled them all. Among them: What if our customer just buys two pills? This did, in fact, happen, but this way it was their idea, not mine, and having war gamed it, they had a Playbook.

By war gaming, you open your mind to the fact that anything can happen. You don't want to find out that your strategies are going to get trumped by the competition and you lose millions of dollars. Winning is the whole premise of doing a war game. This book can help you win. If you want to win, keep reading.

WHAT IS A WAR GAME?

W ar games are a powerful business tool that can accomplish a lot in a relatively short time, but they need to be aligned to key business challenges to be valuable. In situations where the cost of being wrong is high, war games can be very helpful in understanding from a 360-degree perspective the external opportunities and challenges of all the key stakeholders in the industry. War games can also be integrated into existing planning processes and conducted regularly to ensure that a business's understanding of the external environment is regularly evolving.

For war games to be successful, everyone involved should be familiar with a common definition of war games, their process, and the key concepts to understand the benefits. This will ensure that there is alignment about the purpose of war games, recognition of how they work, and understanding of the value they add to business decision-making.

THE DEFINITION OF WAR GAMES IN BUSINESS

War games for business purposes are not about wars nor are they really games. They're enlightening and engaging analytical exercises that can lead to truly creative solutions. War games are structured role-playing workshops used to generate insights to help develop and refine strategy.

War games aren't just dress rehearsals or strategy plans, but are simulations of your competitive market in a controlled, safe, internal environment where you can explore many different dimensions. Ultimately, you build strategies based on actual data points versus going out and spending millions of dollars and learning the hard way that a strategy's not going to work.

Think about weather apps. You open the app and read the forecast for the day. What're the forecasts based upon? In the backend, it's a system of processes with sensors that gather the data, which was run through predictive models that experts built. Are they always accurate? No. However, you get the best guess that they can make based on data and processes. This is similar to war gaming: you make assumptions and run them through a process of established techniques and a transparent framework and come up with data that drives your strategy.

TYPES OF WAR GAMES IN CORPORATIONS

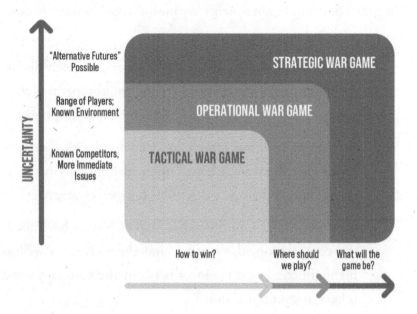

A variety of war-gaming workshops are designed to simulate different future competitive environments, but we will focus on the three main types in this book:

Tactical War Game: How to compete in a specific market against known competitors.

Operational War Game: Where to compete in a changing market with an uncertain set of competitors.

Strategic War Game: How the market is likely to evolve with uncertainty around market structure and competitors.

THE BENEFITS OF WAR GAMES

War games have four main benefits in a business environment because they:

1. create an environment where participants can openly discuss their company's assumptions around the competitive environment and get alignment with their own assumptions;

2. help engage various stakeholders in the decision-making process to collectively achieve buy-in, identify gaps in market knowledge, and create a defensible business strategy;

3. highlight the assumptions that market players have about the competition, the market, and themselves, as well as highlight the key differences between the company's and others' assumptions; and

4. help assess and anticipate potential changes in markets so that a company can predict what other key players are likely to do.

In addition, focused and well-designed war games can help companies to boost their financial performance in three ways:

Risk Identification   **Revenue Generation**   **Cost Avoidance**

1. Risk Identification: Where and how competitive or structural changes in the market threaten to impact companies.

2. Revenue Generation: Where new competitive opportunities arise for companies' existing or new business.

3. Cost Avoidance: How companies can better manage resources relative to how competitors are managing theirs.

CORPORATE USE OF WAR GAMES

CI + War Games are an important business tool used by prominent Global Companies:

Companies have fun war-gaming strategy. Every time I've run a war game in a corporate environment, people get charged up. I built a biotech company's business planning process into a war game. The salespeople got really excited by my bringing in a panel of judges for each round and a leaderboard, possibly because of their innate love of competition. The notion of winning for most gives us that coveted dopamine hit. The engagement increases and everyone buys in, making execution so much easier.

Most pharma and biotech companies do war games because for them, war games are an essential tool to ensure they are making the right decisions when the stakes are high. They spend a billion to a billion and a half dollars and take years to bring a drug to market. As companies in the pharmaceutical industry go through the R&D pipeline, each decision they make gets more and more expensive. For example, at the end of phase II (there are three phases of human testing for pharmaceutical products), they need to make a $200M+ decision as to whether they are ready to commit to a phase III clinical program prior to filing with the FDA. For high-value decisions like these, it makes sense for these companies to make sure that they're heading in the right direction.

P&G | CASE STUDY

Procter & Gamble (P&G) has integrated the war game concept into its core business process. For all major product launches in their industry, they war game. Experienced facilitators coach sales and product development people through each game. This future-oriented intelligence scope provides an outside-in perspective, improves the product development process and product launch timing, involves everyone, and is a powerful risk management tool. Most importantly, it generates more revenue.

Having a future-oriented Intelligence Scope to eliminate surprises

- P&G has institutionalized the War Game concept for all major product launches in the industry.

- Experienced facilitators from MI Team coaches sales and product development people through the game.

- Benefits:
  - Provides an "outside-in" perspective.
  - Improves the product development process and product launch timing.
  - Involves everyone.
  - Risk management tool.
  - Generates more revenue.

Best Practices:

- Integrate war gaming (or other future-oriented analysis methods) into core business processes.

- Keep war gaming topics aligned with business priorities.

When to War Game?

- Significant change in industry landscape.

- Significant change in business strategy.

- Evaluating options in the face of major technology shifts.

- Merger/acquisition decisions.

- Defending vs. new competitor(s).

- Significant change in brand strategy.

- Entering a new market.

- Launching a new product/service.

- Defending against a competitor's new product/service.

IBM | CASE STUDY

IBM calls their war gaming "Competitive Future Threat Assessment Methodology and Process." Their intelligence team delivers highly insightful, deep strategic analysis, which they then workshop in the form of multiple scenarios with key executives, analysts, sales, marketing, and strategy teams. The teams collaborate on an actionable strategy. This approach is much more strategic, as they're using it for the future direction of IBM. It's my understanding that IBM war gamed their reinvention, when they went from being the big blue hardware manufacturer to a systems integrator and consulting firm.

Delivering future-oriented strategic analysis through two-way communication

- IBM's intelligence team has excellent capabilities for delivering highly insightful and deep strategic analysis deliverables.

- Key to their success are methods that enhance two-way communication:
  - Executive workshops
  - Internal & external interviews

- By interacting with its end-users, co-creation of intelligence occurs and user engagement increases.

Best Practices:

- Use workshops and interactive presentations to deliver (and as part of deliverable) strategic deep analysis projects.

- Deliverables are produced collaboratively with executives (co-creation).

Competitive Future Threat Assessment Methodology & Process

RESEARCH

FUTURE THREAT ANALYSIS & CONCLUSIONS

SCENARIO PLANNING & STRATEGY DEVELOPMENT

Baseline financial projections including Geo, Service Line, and Industry Segments
- Thompson First Call Estimates
- Market opportunity projections
- Model assumptions based on deep dive

Deep Dive on competitors' current state & future strategy including Geo, Service Line, and Industry segments
- Financial and industry analyst reports
- Public statements (e.g. press, analysts)
- SME interviews

Findings & Conclusions based on financial projections with assumptions for future strategy/state
- Synthesis of Financial projections and Competitors' Deep Dive
- Leverage knowledge of competitors to create assumptions and predict future state

Identify driving forces, assumptions and uncertainties to build scenarios
- Workshops with key executives, analysts, sales, marketing, and strategy
- Interviews with segment analysts
- Extending FTA findings and conclusions to multiple "what ifs?"

Strategy based on Future Threat Scenarios
- Identify key sign posts to monitor
- Develop strategy that will enable strong competitive position regardless of which scenario comes true

The two previous examples are, of course, large Fortune 500 companies. But you don't have to be the biggest company in a marketplace to win. Building a winning strategy is about creating a strategy that's aligned with your capabilities and the direction that you're heading toward. In the games I run for my students, they inevitably say, "If I'm not on the biggest company's team, I'm going to lose the war game." I tell them that the important thing is building a strategy that makes sense for *you*, as opposed to using another company's Playbook, because every company's reality, resources, and perspectives are different.

ANYONE CAN WAR GAME!

You also don't even have to be a company at all to use war gaming in your daily life. Most of us play *what if* scenarios out in our heads, but don't act upon any of the things we loop about. We go through tortuous intellectual circularity, but never move. This is so common that there is an app for it called ITTT, "If This, Then That." In the app, you create rules based on events; for example, if I upload a list of people and their birthdays, then the app will send them an automatic birthday email. The app takes you out of the planning phase and into the execution phase. With war gaming, you can run through any *what if* scenario and plan for a multitude of *then* outcomes.

I've told a lot of my MBA students who've gotten laid off, "The good thing now is you have time to think, reflect, and game out what your options are versus jumping for the first thing. Because you could get stuck on a path where you may not be happy." I've known so many people in the corporate world say, "I'm going to do this for one year or two years, but my real passion is somewhere else." And then they get stuck. War game to figure out what your passion is.

You can war game your career: What's your objective, or where do you want to be geographically or financially when you're sixty-five years old? What's your winning aspiration? Is it technology? Is it a different industry? What kind of characteristics are there? Now war game backward. Use that to build a plan for your career progression. If you're twenty-five, you've got forty years to achieve your objectives. What do you need to do to get there? Run through the scenarios and measure the outcomes. You can gain knowledge from a longer-term, life-planning perspective.

Then when you look for a job, you won't take the first opportunity that comes along. You know that every time you take an opportunity, you lose three to five years of your life at a minimum because you don't want to be job jumping and become unemployable. If the job you want lists the required skill sets, then how close are you to what they're looking for? If you're weaker than your competition, then how do you make sure you get the job?

In *Alice in Wonderland*, Alice encounters different paths. She asks the Cheshire cat, "Which path should I take?"

He asks back, "Well, where are you trying to get to?"

She answers, "I don't much care where."

He says, "Well, then it doesn't matter which way you go."

The lesson is, if you don't know where you're going, whether you're an individual or a company, then you go nowhere.

CHAPTER 2

BUILDING WINNING STRATEGIES

I n the early nineteenth century, the predominant form of freight and people transportation in the US was railroads. A reporter asked one of the railroad presidents, "What do you think about the airlines?" He quickly responded, "Who cares. We're in a different business." The reporter asked, "So, what business are you in?" He answered, "We're in the railroad business. We're not in the airline business." What he didn't realize was that he was in the transportation business, and so were the airlines. The railroads thought too small— they underestimated their market, and their winning aspiration was narrow. They didn't even see the disruption coming.

Your market is your competitive environment. In other words, it's your war. Your winning aspiration is a goal statement that briefly describes how you'll win your war. It includes your organization's desire, future state, business model, and market. A war game is a single battle, or a moment in time. We all know that wars are fought and won through a series of battles. But, before you battle in a war game, you need to identify your war and what winning means to your company.

To get to your winning aspiration, you'll undergo a cyclical, continuous process, which will be informed by and evolve based on what answers you find in the following chapters. Defining your battlefield, which we do in chapter 7, might change your overall winning aspiration. When you name your competition, which we do in the chapter after that, you might discover some unexpected players in your market, and in turn, your market could expand. Flexibility is imperative, because as you get more information it may change your understanding of what's important versus what's not.

You'll also notice a shifting viewpoint throughout these chapters, where you take a broad look at your company, then you narrow that down into looking at the battle for your war game. I call this a divergent/convergent approach. I will ask you to expand your thinking to include all the factors, then converge or narrow it down to the war game itself. You will also do this in your war game with your team, as you brainstorm ideas and narrow this down into one or two actionable plays.

WHAT WINNING MEANS FOR YOU

The definition of *winning* is different for every company. It's based on each company's realities, structure, resources, culture, and history. Ideally, you have a tight systematic process for defining your winning aspiration that you've been using for a long time and have gotten adept at it. But that doesn't always happen. In some organizations, goals are compromised because there might not be alignment, or the goals may not always be communicated effectively. This can be chaos.

If companies are successful in a particular marketplace, it's for a reason. Sometimes when companies know certain things and this knowledge permeates their culture, they don't realize that for a newcomer, there's a hard learning curve. Another benefit of surveying your market is so you articulate and understand all the different dynamics at play in your business.

YOUR MARKET IS YOUR WAR

Once you define your market in the broadest terms possible, you can set your winning aspiration for the war. Keep in mind that you might be wrong. Look at how your competitor defines their market and compare. In my MBA marketing course, I use a hypothetical example concerning market shares: if Frito-Lay claims a 40 percent market share of potato chips, but Lays, their competitor, claims a 10 percent share of salty snacks—salty snacks being a far bigger market as it includes pretzels and nuts. Now the game changes, because Frito-Lay limited their playing field by not playing the same game as their competitor. This happens in a marketplace all the time where companies define their market in too narrow of a way, so they end up playing on the wrong field.

ASPIRATIONAL OR POSITIONAL WINNING

Winning can be two things: It can be aspirational, i.e., where you want to end up. If you're not there, then the bigger question is the following: How do you get there? Are you doing the right kind of activities to bridge the gap between where you are right now and where your aspirations lie? Or it could be positional, i.e., holding your top spot. If you're already winning, then the question is how do you continue to maintain your leadership in this space, and continue to be successful?

I mentioned Blockbuster already, but their positional winning aspiration was to be the number one DVD rental company. They got to the top spot and got too comfortable. Complacency happens with a lot of established companies. They get market leadership and believe nobody can topple them. But one hungry startup with a huge aspiration comes along and topples them.

When Amazon launched their business, do you think they defined their market as secondhand book selling? They might have. But if they kept it that way, they would still be a secondhand bookstore. At some point, they changed that definition, expanding their winning aspiration and their market with it. The secondhand bookstore was a stepping-stone to becoming a firsthand bookstore and then to becoming the largest e-commerce book seller.

At some point, their winning aspiration grew bigger. Amazon wanted to be the largest retail e-commerce website. They went deep into the books vertical and then replicated that in verticals, branching out until they became sellers of everything.

However, they didn't stop at that. They opened their systems to other retailers and became the world's largest marketplace.

Today, Amazon's aspiration is not about selling products. It's now about capturing customer data, a far more valuable commodity.

FUTURE-FORWARD ASPIRATIONS

Apple, when they began, was called "Apple Computer Inc." Their original logo wasn't even an Apple. It was Sir Isaac Newton sitting under the apple tree. This method of branding is what happens when you get a bunch of engineers together who say, "Hey, build a logo or build some marketing stuff." In 2007, Apple got rid of "Computer Company," when they expanded into consumer electronics and became just Apple.

Their biggest competitor, Microsoft, believes that controlling the software is where the value is. They never really produced hardware, which is a different winning aspiration than Apple. Apple's winning aspiration is controlling the whole user experience, so they define their business as software and hardware in an integrated ecosystem.

Apple struggled for a while because that approach was too niche at first, although widely embraced by creative people. When I bought my first Mac computer in the late 2000s, my brother asked me, "Why did you buy a Mac? You're not an engineer or an architect or a musician, right? What are you going to do with it?" Then, suddenly the mainstream market changed due to advances in technology and the internet and opened to everyone. Their winning aspiration came to fruition as the market changed.

POSITIONAL ASPIRATIONS AND MARKET EXPANSION

Starbucks Coffee began in 1971 as a coffee bean seller in Seattle's Pike Place Market. They went from selling a commodity to becoming the largest coffee company in the world. But how? Their winning aspiration might have started with providing the best beans in their neighborhood, but to stay ahead of the hyper competitive Seattle coffee market they kept expanding: the best beans to the best cup of coffee, to more locations for convenience and consistency. Now their positional aspiration is to serve everyone in the world the same tasting cup of coffee. Starbucks has been expanding steadily for decades. You can find a Starbucks coffee on almost every corner in every city in the US, and in almost every country in the world, aside from Cuba, Pakistan, Iran, and Croatia.[3]

EXAMPLES OF WINNING ASPIRATIONS

Equinox: Physical gyms and experiential luxury fitness

Peloton: Replicating the gym experience at home

American Airlines: The largest airline in the world

Southwest Airline: Low-cost options for consumers

Emirates: Contributing to the Dubai economy

Qatar: Building a world-class airline

British Airways: Dominate the Transatlantic channel

Frontier & Spirit: Low cost, smaller scale

BMW: Performance. Be the ultimate driving machine

Volvo: Safety

Toyota: Mass market

Porsche: High-end luxury

---

3   Kristine Hansen, "12 Places around the world where Starbucks is banned, shunned, or basically unsuccessful," Fodors Travel Guide, March 30, 2023, https://www.fodors.com/news/photos/places-around-the-world-where-starbucks-is-banned.

WAR GAMING YOUR WINNING ASPIRATION

If you have a winning aspiration but aren't sure if it's relevant, want to expand it, or need to get internal alignment on it; you've got a lot of work to do. If you're struggling with this exercise, war games can help you because they're forward thinking, an area in which traditional analysis is weak.

Some leadership teams have great alignment and focus. They've defined their business objectives, articulated winning aspirations for the long and short terms, as well as created a Playbook for initiatives to achieve their goals. Then that all gets cascaded down into the departments, and then into projects with rules or standards that state all projects have aligned with the initiatives in the Playbook. And if it doesn't, then nobody can do it.

Other companies just go around in circles. The senior executives talk among themselves about winning aspirations, etc., but middle management is wondering what they're saying, because it's radically different from the reality on the ground. When planners plan in isolation, the organization finds itself dealing with discontinuities and lack of synthesis.

In a best-case scenario, you have alignment and a clear vision of where you're heading. So, you stress test it in a war game to see if you're thinking through it the right way or not. In a worst-case scenario, you don't have alignment, but you know it needs to be fixed. And, of course, there's everything in between.

CALCULATE YOUR PLANNING HORIZON

Your planning horizon is how long you're going to engage in the war, or just the next battle. Growth is a huge driver for companies;

growth at all costs. But there's a big difference between organic and exponential growth. Organic growth can be said as follows: *Let's just book the next deal, then the next, and the next, and then we'll kind of go from there.* But if you want exponential growth and to have a deliberate vision for the future, then determining your planning horizons (short- and long-term) will help you.

For example, Dubai went from being a very small town in the Middle East to being a huge financial center because of the founders' long-term aspiration. Their aspiration was to move people, freight, and money easily. They built the infrastructure—hotels, regulatory frameworks, etc., and people asked them: "What are you building for? There's nothing there." But they kept on, and Dubai is a regional magnet for finance, trade, and commerce, and now a lot of people are moving there also.

Singapore also had a long-term planning horizon and a very deliberate strategy. The city was the poorest part of Malaysia, and the prime minister went on TV to announce that the country was declaring independence from the Malaysian Federation. The city government created a very deliberate long-term planning horizon for their strategy. They built an island nation, which is now one of the richest in the world. They have the most favorable passport in terms of travel documents. Now people from Malaysia are trying to come and work in Singapore.

Broadly speaking, planning horizons are either short or long term, but the length varies according to the industry. If you're in the oil and gas industry, you've got hundreds of millions of dollars in investments, and you must deal with local politics where you want to drill, so your timeframe's a lot longer, usually about thirty years for long term and five to ten years for short term. If you're in the technology industry, you can't even plan for thirty years. Long-term planning horizons for tech might be six months, and short-term might be tomorrow.

But beware! That doesn't mean companies with shorter planning horizons shouldn't plan at all. Some companies are narrowly focused on what to do for the next three months, and that's it. If they're so busy executing and don't take time to think about where they're headed, they can end up misdirecting heavy resources toward something that might not help them in the long term. A lot of tech companies who have paused for a day or two for war games have realized if they take a more holistic and longer-term view of their business, they end up with a much more productive and profitable outcome.

In this chapter, we talked about how your company wants to win in your market, e.g., *my company wants to capture 40 percent of the market share.* In the next, we explore the core attributes any company needs to achieve competitive success.

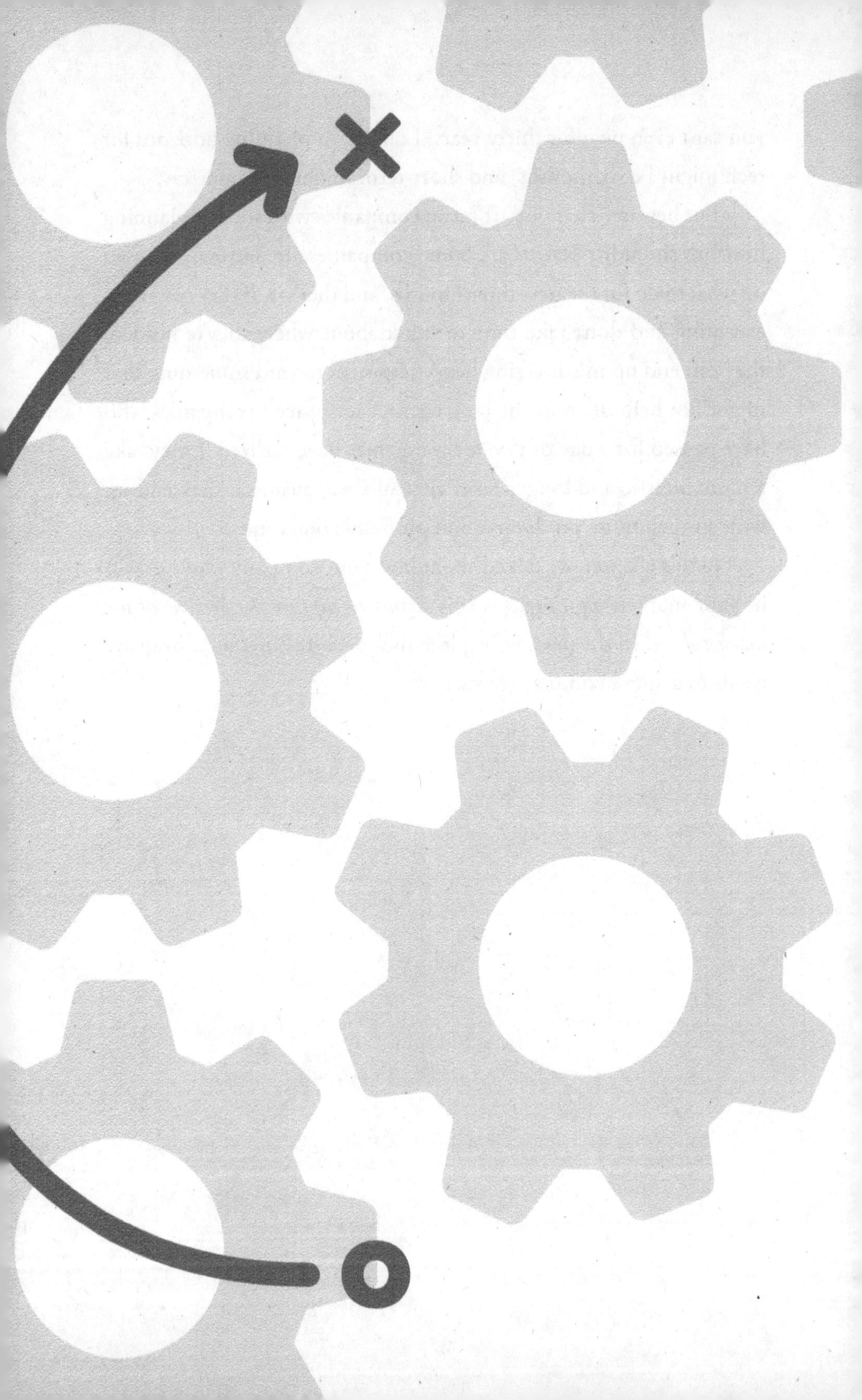

CORE ATTRIBUTES FOR COMPETITIVE SUCCESS

B ack in the late 1990s, a well-known consultancy ran a war game for an aircraft manufacturing client who was thinking of competing for a Department of Defense (DoD) contract to produce a supersonic jet against Boeing Corp, McDonnell Douglas, and Northrup. Competing for government contracts is a multi-million-dollar venture that takes years to come to fruition, but the payoff is in the billions. It made sense to war game the strategy before attempting to throw their hat in the ring. After running the simulation, Boeing Corp was the clear winner. The client wasn't having it.

They asked the consultant to run the game again.

The Boeing team won.

They asked for a third war game.

Again, Boeing won the contract.

After three games, the aircraft manufacturer finally asked, *Why?* They had the best technology and engineering of all their competitors and were confident they could design a far superior jet. The answer is: the government wasn't looking for innovation; it was looking for the lowest price possible. Boeing, with no experience in defense aircraft, bid the lowest.

The aircraft manufacturer did proceed to bid on the contract, but still lost to Boeing.[4] While war games are not a magical crystal ball in predicting the future, they do give greater insight into what is likely to happen. And, once a war game points out a clear strategy, it's up to the company to execute.

Over my years of consulting, I've noticed a pattern with successful companies who have the right winning characteristics. I call these the ten attributes for competitive success, which you can apply to any industry. These ten characteristics in their entirety make the difference between a mediocre company and a profitable, healthy enterprise. War gaming will help any company or individual attain all of these.

The war game helped us develop a strategy to compete in a new market... we refer to the playbook from the war game almost every day.

—TA HEAD, RARE DISEASE FRANCHISE TOP 10 PHARMACEUTICAL COMPANY

---

4   Mark Lawson, "War games give execs a piece of the action," *The Australian Financial Review*, January 1998.

1. EMBRACING AND LEARNING FROM FAILURE

In general, corporate America's lack of acknowledgment of failure is terrifying. Successful companies encounter failure with a let's-learn-from-it attitude, instead of brushing it aside.

For this attribute, I'm referring to two kinds of failure: Thinking you know and failing and not knowing and failing. Either way, in war gaming the whole point is to simulate failure. In a safe war-gaming simulation, you can use failure as a springboard to succeed. It's much less painful and cheaper to fail in a workshop than to deploy millions of dollars to find out afterward it's not going to work.

One example of a company that failed on both counts was Nokia. This multi-billion-dollar cell phone company knew their market was changing, but they failed to respond and adapt. They had access to competitive intelligence which indicated Apple, Samsung, and other smart phone manufacturers were coming to market. They did nothing and argued, "We're number one in the marketplace. We've got more than 40 percent market share. All these other companies don't know the mobile space like we do."

They also failed due to what they didn't know. They thought that nobody could replicate a desktop computing experience on the mobile phone, because the screen of real estate was too small. And we all know how that turned out.

Companies willing to learn from failures or potential failures are the ones that tend to be more successful. In war gaming, you ideate any failures (How do we get out of this? What if our product doesn't get approved? What if our tech stack fails? What if the economy collapses?) and instead of ignoring them, you have honest conversations in order to arrive at actionable, winning competitive strategies.

2. MAKING QUICKER DECISIONS AND FAST EXECUTION

In our global, fast-moving economy, being quicker than your competition in terms of decisions and execution are both keys to success. Fail or succeed, but above all, move fast. I understand why most companies get analysis paralysis: they fear making decisions until they have all the information. What they don't realize is that they will never have 100 percent of the data.

The only way anyone can predict something is 100 percent going to happen is *after* it's happened. *The Wall Street Journal* reports on what already happened with accuracy. But if you run a business, you can't innovate and stay ahead of the competition if you make decisions based on only historical data. Innovation requires that you rely on less-than-certain information and act quickly, which always carries an element of risk.

Agile companies execute based on less certainty. To be agile you need to be comfortable with making decisions when you have incomplete information. This is risk taking. And it, too, can lead to failure: you thought you knew, but you were wrong.

With war gaming, you can make quick decisions and execute on the fly because you've taken limited, uncertain information and turned it into something far more certain. Companies that war game risky decisions test their assumptions within a safe environment and make a clear plan to move forward. By testing your hypotheses, you can mitigate risk, as this gives you greater certainty. Based on the outcome, you can move fast with your Playbook and buy-in from key stakeholders.

3. THINKING GLOBALLY, ACTING LOCALLY

In a global economy, the barriers to marketplace entry are all but gone. We've gone from proprietary expertise to easily and inexpensively replicable systems. Computing is one example. Years ago, the infrastructure and equipment for computing were available only to multinational companies, who had the resources to spend millions for hardware and custom programs. Now, companies can get a software subscription for a few hundred dollars a month and access to huge systems they wouldn't have been able to come close to fifty years ago. For example, Odoo is an open-source SaaS in the Bay Area. For about $25 a month per user companies can build an IT infrastructure—everything from accounting to marketing to CRM, to shipping, inventory—all of it on the cloud.

With war gaming, if you've got a global value proposition, you can customize scenarios for the local markets you want to get into. For example, when McDonald's wanted to launch in India, they didn't launch with a Big Mac because 80 percent of the population is Hindu. While this is common knowledge, sometimes local customs can be harder to discern, unless you've explored all the details in a war game.

Tesco,[5] Europe's largest grocery chain, tried to open tiny self-service stores in the US in 2006, which they called "Fresh & Easy." By 2012, the chain pulled out of the US at a $2 billion loss. With a war game, they could have avoided a string of costly mistakes, all due to a misunderstanding of the different regions in the US. By introducing stores that American consumers, accustomed to full-time unionized

---

5 "International expansion: Why Tesco missed the mark in the U.S. market: Insights," CASTUS, September 12, 2022, https://www.castusglobal.com/insights/international-expansion-why-tesco-missed-the-mark-in-the-u-s-market.

grocery cashiers and bulk purchases,[6] didn't understand, they were forced to leave the market.

You can war game scenarios for every region or country you want to enter, exploring the unique cultural differences and tailoring your offerings to fit. This is the best way to ensure competitive success in new markets.

4. DEFINING YOUR BUSINESS AND SETTING GOALS

War gaming can help companies find themselves by broadening their business scope and setting winning, lofty aspirations. I've seen many companies come into a war game for these two different outcomes. War games help them ask themselves the right questions, define themselves, and set winning aspirations:

1. Redefining goals: The company who knows their market is changing but doesn't know how to position themselves within it. They war game to factor in their evolving competitive environment, government regulations, or any other external forces that are forcing them to reassess their business.

2. Goal setting: The leadership team wants to pressure test a new, bigger goal that they aren't sure about unless they can simulate how the competition will challenge them, or how a new market will respond.

How does Uber define its business? Is it to get a customer from point A to point B or is there a bigger play? Uber defines itself as a Mobility as a Service (MaaS) business, with a goal of getting everyone and everything from point A to point B by any means (car, helicopter,

---

6   "Why did Tesco fail in the US?" September 17, 2021, https://www.vertexresourcing.com/blog/2020-08-tesco-fail-in-the-us.

drone, bikes, etc.). Like I mentioned before, if Amazon had defined its business as just a bookstore, they would still be a bookstore. Amazon defined its business as collecting customer data and set a goal to use it for whatever purposes they needed.

For some companies, their self-definition and goals are explicit. And their journeys are easier as they have clear paths. But other companies struggle with lower aspirations and get stuck on circular paths, not really heading in any direction but just going around and around. They must undergo a process of finding themselves. War gaming helps do this.

5. OFFERING A UNIQUE VALUE PROPOSITION

What is your company's unique value proposition, i.e., something that you have that no one else can offer? Before you answer, think about this: A unique value proposition doesn't mean that your product or service must be the only one on the market. For example, why does the Apple MacBook have a price point of $1,500–$2,000, whereas Google Chromebooks cost $300? Both manufacturers have access to the same raw material suppliers. The same thing can be illustrated by a Michelin star restaurant versus a roadside diner, both with the same food supplier. In most industries, you have access to the same raw materials (not just physical resources but also skills and talent) that your competition does. The unique value is in how each maker puts their offer together.

In war gaming, when a company is considering several unique value propositions, we divide their players up into competing teams and put them in front of a panel comprising real or mock customers. Then we challenge the teams to sell their value propositions to the "customers." The panel then gives each team a score from one to ten. Then they ask the panel why they found one proposition more agreeable than another and fine-tune it from the customer's perspective.

What does the value proposition have to look like? Ask yourself these questions:

- What are my customers looking for in every market I serve?

- How do those markets look different from each other?

- Where's the gap in each market?

- Is anyone else supporting that gap or not?

- And if not, where is the opportunity?

- Where's the bigger opportunity?

- How can we meet the customer's needs more proactively and quicker than our competitors?

6. BANKING ON A SOLID REPUTATION AND ETHICS

Reputation and ethics really go hand-in-hand. Gone are the days of just selling cigarettes without impunity. Now tobacco companies must think about carcinogens in their products, the environment, and the effects of their products on society. Of course, we still have companies that do the bare minimum not just for regulatory compliance but for public relations, like the waitress in the movie "Office Space" who was required to have seven buttons to meet her "flair" quota. Companies need to go beyond marketing speak and prove their reputations through responsible actions and accountability.

The most successful companies are authentic. They are genuinely concerned about corporate ethics, make strategic choices, and cross-check their strategies against what does the least harm or does the greatest good. Those organizational cultures end up being a lot more successful. The trick is in reading the room, so to speak, or understanding that your decisions carry reputational risk, whether it's your marketing strategy, your hiring practices, your supply chain transparency, or your labor practices. The consumer voice is influencing how American and even foreign corporations conduct themselves in the US market, and the government is responding.

For example, the US Federal Trade Commission (FTC) and US Food and Drug Administration (FDA) in the first quarter of 2023 issued warning letters to over 600 supplement manufacturers questioning their active ingredients and health claims due to consumer complaints. In the supplement industry, some manufacturers make claims, based on a single ingredient, that their products will improve customers' health without clinically testing their formulations. Consumer watchdog organizations, like the Clean Label Project, batch test supplements for purity and potency and have found ingredients like toxic metals, pesticides, and poisonous compounds in products that claim to be 100 percent natural, not to mention dosages that are far below or above the claims on the label. This entire industry, dubbed "snake oil," is undergoing a renaissance due to market and regulatory pressure.

War gaming is useful when regulatory changes are on the horizon. When a company isn't sure how these changes will affect their business, good or bad, war gaming helps clarify this. Often, through war gaming, a company can see an opportunity to change for the better and in doing so, distinguishes itself in a crowded market.

7. FOCUSING ON CUSTOMERS

A lot of companies talk about being customer focused, saying "our customer is king" or "we think about our customers," but do they really mean it? I conducted a war game for one of the largest logistics companies in the world, and at the end of two days I asked them a question:

"Guys, why are you in business?"

They answered, "For our customers."

I told them, "In the last two days, how many times in this room full of thirty-five senior execs did any of you hear the word 'customer'?"

They all suddenly realized that they didn't hear or say that word even once. They would have benefited in bringing in customer perspectives into the war game, but also into their business.

I spoke about bringing a panel of judges posing as customers into a war game in my fifth point above.

This type of war game is about getting feedback. Build your value proposition, and always present it to your customers to see what the feedback is. If they say it's terrible, go back and do something differently. This is the best early indicator of success. You can also bring other entities in like influencers or key opinion leaders to your industry; for example, in pharmaceuticals you could bring in doctors, analysts, and journalists to provide feedback.

8. LEARNING FROM THE COMPETITION

Companies that fail don't want to know anything about their competitors because they don't respect them. Companies that succeed have an open mind and wish to learn from the competition, even though their competitors might not be as strong. They know anything can change significantly in an ever-evolving market.

Walmart's expansion into Germany is a perfect example of how the massive chain vastly underestimated the local butcher and lost in a classic David and Goliath stand-off. Walmart used the same strategy for opening stores in the US for its German expansion, but they underestimated the local competition, whom they didn't even see as a threat. For example, they opened stores in unwalkable districts, whereas the local butcher set up shop right around the corner. Also, they greeted shoppers at the door with a smile, but local people took that as an imposition, as they only greet people they know with a smile (e.g., the local butcher). Finally, they sold prepackaged items under their own brand, including meat, which Germans never buy. Instead, they prefer fresh cuts from, you guessed it, the local butcher. After unsuccessfully attempting to break into the German market for ten years, they gave up. The lesson here is, of course, get to know your local market, but also don't underestimate your competition, no matter how small.[7]

The whole idea of war gaming in a traditional sense is learning from your competitors, or competitive intelligence, which I will go more into detail later in the book.

9. MAXIMIZING SKILL SETS AND PLAYING AS A TEAM

I've had a few corporations say, "We want to do a war game. This is our situation: We're going to strategize X, Y, and Z." And after thinking about it, it was clear they were not ready to do a strategic game because they weren't integrated—they were barely talking to each other.

---

[7]   Samantha Yoder, John K. Visich, Elzotbek Rustambekov, "Lessons learned from international expansion failures and successes," *Kelly School of Business* 59, (2015): 233–43.

But what I have suggested is that those companies use a war game to integrate their teams. A client, one of the largest travel companies in the US, took me up on this. They wanted to war game for two goals: The first war game would be around team building for their leadership; and following that they would test new strategies in the post-COVID-19 world. They knew they needed to build a unified team before they went into battle, and they did this with success.

Team building is a softer attribute, but it's also very important for successful companies. Having a strong functional team with the right skill sets, background, and attitude is key to success. Granted, you're always going to have turf wars in any company, but if you can put them aside to work collaboratively toward a goal, you can win.

War gaming also helps leaders see the kinds of resources they have in the room and helps them understand what skill sets they need in order to execute. I've also had instances where the more senior person involved in the war game has told me in confidence that they are also using the exercise to determine whom to promote based on how they can present strategies, defend, and lead teams.

10. INNOVATING TO WIN

Every company wants to be the originator of The Next Big Thing. But if you look at success, as an organization, you don't have to create or have original ideas, as I explained in the fifth point about unique value proposition. Innovation can also be doing the same thing as your competition but doing it better or quicker. The innovation can be your strategy, or Playbook.

Facebook rarely has had original ideas—just look at their history. The way that they innovated was to take over one university at a time and build an intranet community on each campus. The idea wasn't original, as MySpace and Friendster were already well established, but they executed in a truly innovative way, adding better features, no ads, and faster load times.[8] All the other expansions that they've had since have been acquired: WhatsApp, Instagram, Oculus, and now artificial intelligence (AI). They purchase innovative companies rather than re-invent the products they want.

I've seen many companies war game an innovative execution plan, get alignment, check off the right skill sets, and kill the competition even though the competition has a better product.

Now that you know what it takes to win, I will show you in the next chapter why war gaming is better than traditional planning, sharing stories of companies who either failed with the latter, or succeeded with the former.

---

8   Evan Tarver, "3 social media networks before Facebook," Investopedia, September 13, 2022, https://www.investopedia.com/articles/markets/081315/3-social-media-networks-facebook.asp.

HOW IS WAR GAMING BETTER THAN TRADITIONAL PLANNING?

D o you remember Boeing's Dreamliner 787 versus the double-decker Airbus A380? Both companies made two very different bets in the marketplace. Boeing strategized based on external data such as rising gas prices, and impatient customers that wanted to fly non-stop rather than get stranded in a hub city. Boeing created the smaller, lighter Dreamliner out of high-tech composites, to seat around 300 people. The fuel-efficient Dreamliner is ideal for international routes and quickly became a best seller.[9]

Airbus made a very different bet, dependent on the airlines continuing to transport people from hub to hub. To appeal to the airlines, but more likely just to stroke their own egos, they created a 600-person, luxury, double-decker engineering marvel. The Airbus turned

---

9   Robert Wall and Daniel Michaels, "How Airbus's A380 went from wonder to blunder," WSJ.com, February 19, 2019, https://www.wsj.com/articles/how-airbuss-a380-went-from-wonder-to-blunder-11550599532.

out to be too big for most airports. People didn't want to fly with 600 other people or go from hub to hub, and gas prices soared through the roof. As a result, they've been in and out of production since the early 2000s, limiting themselves to hub-based international airlines like Emirates and Singapore, which cater to high-end customers.

Airbus used traditional planning, starting off with a situational analysis (leadership wanted a bigger, quieter and more luxurious plane) and working down to the financial objectives and budgeting. This type of planning misses a 360-degree perspective of the external environment, as it doesn't take the customer or competition into account.

War gaming, on the other hand, is that 360-degree external assessment that you need. The game is designed around how to differentiate your business in a way that no one else can replicate it. War gaming gives you an understanding of your external environment: your customers and their value drivers; your competition and, even better, *all* the other stakeholders in your marketplace (regulatory government agencies, supply chains) which are usually ignored in traditional planning.

A lot of times companies like Airbus that undergo traditional planning lose sight of the customer. The customers are an afterthought. And with tactical war games, especially, you can bring the customer to the forefront, asking the following questions: Who is your customer? What do they want? How are you going to connect and sell to them better than your competition?

Depending on the organization, traditional planning is a standard methodology comprising anywhere from three to eight steps. It typically starts off with a situational analysis and moves into strategic themes, strategic imperatives, and then ultimately cascades down to building and budgeting. Companies that run on a calendar year will usually kick it off in February, and it'll be in place by October for the following year. This calendar-based approach is one dimensional, in that you're solely looking at your organization.

In some instances, you'll see a market overview used as a place-holder on a hastily created slide that functions as a tick mark that they've investigated, but there's not much more thought to it, and that is the main problem. Traditional planning has many pitfalls, which I will go into below with examples of companies that could've won had they used war-gaming strategy. To begin, below is a summary of the core differences.

I have been to many previous games but this one is by far the best I have attended...I have a playbook I can plug directly into my launch plan...

—EUROPEAN BRAND LEAD RESPONSIBLE FOR
LAUNCHING A BLOCKBUSTER IN 2016

TRADITIONAL PLANNING VERSUS WAR GAMING

Most organizations plan like this:

- Forecast a linear extrapolation of past trends

  □ "The world will be a little different"

- Do you want to make bets based on absurdly low probabilities?

  □ A forecast dependent on 30 events, each 80% likely, provides a ~0.1% chance of success

Even though the world looks like this:

- Discontinuous change

  - Complex interaction of many forces, some known, many unknown

- Great uncertainity

- Any plan must be dynamic and evolutionary

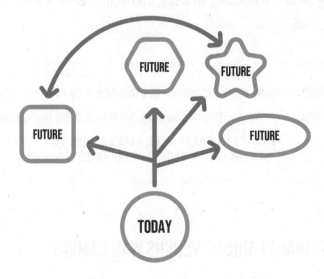

Traditional planning differs from war gaming in three basic ways:[10]

1. *Internal versus external thinking:* Traditional planning addresses a linear timeline and a stable market that everyone is well familiar with. War gaming addresses the uncertainty of a changing market, or the *what-ifs* that traditional planning can't account for.

---

10 Micah Zenko and Maryam Shariati, "What if you had red teamed?" McChrystal Group, March 2023, https://www.mcchrystalgroup.com/insights/what-if-you-had-red-teamed/.

2. *Top-down versus bottom-up decision-making:* Traditional planning is a decision handed down by one or more stakeholders and doesn't invite input from all key stakeholders, as does war gaming. This makes it difficult or impossible to execute the plan, as the leadership hands it over to inexperienced managers, or managers who do not buy in.

3. *Internal bias goes unchallenged:* In traditional planning, the executives might have inherent bias, denial, or be ignorant of the external world. Unchallenged, they proceed to the disaster of the organization. War gaming invites challenges to leadership's assumptions.

THROWING STUFF AT THE WALL

Some companies don't have an effective decision-making process, a department for strategy, or even decision-making training for employees. In this case, the strategies they make are compromises, cobbled together in bits and pieces and thrown at a wall in the hopes that something sticks. *We'll sell some more stuff, we'll do this, and a little of that.* It's not much more sophisticated than that.

BIC is a good example of a company that demonstrates the inconsistency of traditional planning. All companies have wins and losses, but when you see how bizarre their outputs are, it's clear that this company doesn't war game when releasing new products. They've had great success with lighters, pens, and even temporary tattoos and sticky notes, but once they got into disposable panties, pens just for women, and perfume, they lost millions of dollars. One writer noted about BIC's successes and failures, "But if you lose your focus on what made your company truly innovative, and try to sell products to a consumer base you don't fully understand, or fall for cheap marketing ploys, you'll be throwing money down the drain."[11]

In traditional planning, you end up with a plan that you've never tested. You're still going out into the Wild Wild West when you don't even know if the plan is going to work, especially when you aren't taking the customer into account, which brings us to the next example.

IGNORING THE CUSTOMER

Lululemon indisputably created the athleisure market. Despite an incredible amount of success at the beginning of their launch, it soon became apparent that Lululemon had a very narrow customer type with a fit body shape, to the detriment of everyone else, when they released a sheer yoga pant that customers complained loudly about. Addressing the backlash, Lululemon founder Chip Wilson told Bloomberg TV that "Frankly, some women's bodies don't actually work" for their pants. Their stock fell 20 percent after that comment. CEO Christine Day advised customers to "bend over in the fitting room" to see if they were sheer. She was fired, as was the Head of Product. Finally, after investors brought a lawsuit against Lululemon, the founder issued an apology, and the company recalled the pants ($20 million lost) and released a newer model that boasted extra fabric in the rear. But the damage had been done and it took the company some time to recover.[12]

---

11   Aytekin Tank, "This entrepreneur pitfall is a primal impulse," Entrepreneur, January 24, 2020, https://www.entrepreneur.com/growing-a-business/this-entrepreneur-pitfall-is-a-primal-impulse/345246.

12   Aaron Smith, "Lululemon sued for see-through yoga pants," CNNMoney, July 3, 2013, https://money.cnn.com/2013/07/03/news/companies/lululemon-yoga-lawsuit/index.html.

A lot of times companies with traditional planning lose sight of the customer. Customers are an afterthought. With war gaming, you can bring the customer to the forefront; especially in those tactical games where you can really run scenarios that give insight into your market.

It's easy in the case with Lululemon to see where leadership failed, and then some outside consultancy or agency helped them clean up their image and attempt to make things right. But hiring consultants in the front end can also cause a lot of headaches.

BLAMING THE CONSULTANTS

The problem with hiring consultants for traditional strategy is that nobody has skin in the game. What ends up happening in a lot of instances is the people that sell the project aren't the ones that execute it. The ones to execute that strategy are inexperienced staff without industry perspective or experience. When the consultants' strategy inevitably doesn't go right, executives blame the consultants, so everyone can keep their jobs. One *Business Insider* author writes, "Consultants create their answers, and then leave… Effectively we have a great strategy but because of the way it was formed (they went off and thought about it and came back with an answer) we can't execute it."[13]

I met a CFO last week who had hired one of the Big Three to consult with his company. He told me, "That was the worst money I spent in the last two years of being a CFO. If I could, I would ask for a refund from that organization."

---

13 Nilofer Merchant, Yes, And Know…, "Why we all hate consultants (and why it's okay)," *Business Insider*, February 14, 2010, https://www.businessinsider.com/why-we-all-hate-consultants-and-why-its-okay-2011-6.

By doing a war game, the ownership is there. Ultimately, the outputs in a war game are the outputs of the participants. You get alignment in terms of the perspective. You break down the thought process and what your actions are going to be coming out of it.

Let's say you don't want to outsource your strategy but prefer to keep it in-house, as your leadership has the context that a consultant would lack. This can also be a pitfall without a war-gaming strategy.

TRUSTING ONE DECISION-MAKER

Excite, a search engine company run by George Bell, was given the chance, by Larry Page, to purchase Google for $750k, and a 1 percent stake in Excite. Bell passed. Why he passed depends on whom you ask. If you ask George Bell, he passed because he didn't see how Google was any better than his product, and he didn't like Larry Page's ask: that Google replace Excite. If you ask an employee at the time, Steven Levy, he writes in his book *In the Plex* that Bell didn't like that Google was faster, and that the goal for Excite at the time was to keep people on their page so that they would see all of their ads. If the customers were given the results as quickly as they were with Google, he theorized, they would bounce. Either way, the decision as to whether to buy Google came down to one person: George Bell.

His reasons for passing seem quite reasonable, if you look at it from a traditional strategy point of view. Why would Bell disrupt his own successful business for this newcomer? He employed hundreds of engineers. His investors were big fans. Stay the course and you'll be successful. In a linear sense, he was sure to win.

If he had war gamed, he would have challenged his own assumptions instead of justifying them. He would have looked at the market and the customer. He might have seen that his customers *wanted* fast, accurate results. And that Google's technology served that need. He could have re-thought his business model. Even if he still believed Excite was better, he would have at the very least gobbled up potential competition for a steal and given himself time to think about his next move. By mitigating risk with a war game, his company would today, like Google, be worth over one trillion dollars.[14]

If one person making all the decisions is a problem, the next example shows us how a team of untrained decision-makers can be just as detrimental.

BEING TOO SLOW TO MAKE DECISIONS

Back when tiny phones were seen as the height of tech (who can forget Zoolander's stupidly minuscule flip phone?), the 2006 Motorola Razr dominated the mobile phone market at over 22 percent market share.

Why did they fail to release a smartphone or innovate? The consensus is that Motorola senior management was slow and inexperienced.[15] Their strategy again was traditional: if something works, don't change it. So, they sat back and enjoyed their market share, for a short year, then started selling off their phones at a discount in 2007, as they were already obsolete.

Tech moves fast, and Motorola simultaneously started and slept through the phone revolution. Leadership didn't decide to release a new product until 2010! Four years is like a century in tech, so they

---

14   Brian McCullough, "The real reason Excite turned down buying Google for $750,000 in 1999," *Internet History Podcast*, November 17, 2014, https://www.internethistorypodcast.com/2014/11/the-real-reason-excite-turned-down-buying-google-for-750000-in-1999/.

15   Howard Anderson, "10 Reasons why Motorola failed," Network World, April 9, 2008, https://www.networkworld.com/article/2277903/10-reasons-why-motorola-failed.html.

were disastrously late, having to pit an outdated Razr against the iPhone and the Blackberry.

War games wake up your leadership from complacency and prepare them for these kinds of attacks. It's like building a future radar of your environment in a systematic manner, and it helps to calibrate the attention of your team to the signals in the marketplace. War games ensure that you're building strategies based on what's happening in the marketplace, versus just building something and then later discovering that it was wrong. Those are all elements that are not in traditional planning. We've seen so many examples of companies that have been doing that, not just Motorola.

It's one thing to say, "Hey, we're going to be number one in this market." But then you've got to take a hard look and ask, do we have the cultural embedding for it to work? You get this from war gaming. Again, organizations don't typically put their leadership through decision-maker training, which leads to large fluctuations in decision quality. You start having a lot more bad decisions than high-quality ones, because no decision is still a decision.

Making a plan is one thing, and executing the plan is another. Traditional planning can get you sound strategy up to a point, but for execution it's a miss. This leads us to the next point.

LACKING THE ABILITY TO EXECUTE

Traditional planning can give you an excellent strategy, but it doesn't give your leadership a Playbook for how to execute it. Nor does it motivate your team to be able to do it. The strategy may not be aligned with what your inherent goals are, but you have no way to test or challenge that in a traditional environment.

Kodak is one example of failure that has had experts weighing in for years about what went wrong: how they failed to innovate, or they failed to anticipate market changes. Yet, the facts remain that Kodak was an early adopter of cutting-edge digital technology; they knew change was coming and invested heavily into it. Quite simply, they failed to execute.

Everything Kodak did was so close, but not quite. An analysis done by Harvard Business Review regarding Kodak's failure concluded:

> The right lessons from Kodak are subtle. Companies often see the disruptive forces affecting their industry. They frequently divert sufficient resources to participate in emerging markets. Their failure is usually an inability to embrace the new business models the disruptive change opens up. Kodak created a digital camera, invested in the technology, and even understood that photos would be shared online. Where they failed was in realizing that online photo sharing *was* the new business, not just a way to expand the business.[16]

BLOWING THE WHISTLE

The cost of failure at the start of a project is much cheaper than once you've sunk hundreds of millions of dollars in. The more money sinks in, the more vested you are for its success. But what happens if you've gated your strategy from the rest of the organization and delivered it, but someone in your organization, acting as the whistleblower, doesn't agree? In most companies, that person would be typecast as the naysayer, and "not a team player." Nobody wants to be that person,

16 Scott D. Anthony, "Kodak's downfall wasn't about technology," *Harvard Business Review*, April 24, 2017, https://hbr.org/2016/07/kodaks-downfall-wasnt-about-technology.

and besides, most rationalize, the plan is already in place so it's too late.

But in a safe (non-costly) war-gaming environment, everyone is invited to blow the whistle, if only to get over a fear of failure. It's not too late at that point to poke holes in the strategy.

What does anyone have to lose if they bring a potential problem out into the open so that everyone can talk about if it makes sense? You eliminate fear of failure by really facing it.

War games help in situations where there's fear of failure in your organization. Who knows—maybe Kodak was paralyzed because they were afraid of disrupting their core business. Perhaps they were uncomfortable with doing something unfamiliar. War gaming would have given the entire organization alignment around what their course of actions would be.

NOT ALIGNING AS A TEAM

Getting alignment on a strategy is important and one of the biggest challenges in any organization. You get alignment in war games because the players create the outputs, so they have ownership. They can't argue or whistle blow when they created the plan themselves. One of the things I do with war-gaming Playbooks is to make sure they contain photographs of the game, for example, pictures of teams writing strategies on a whiteboard. It's a reminder that they've ideated and approved the strategy, so they own it and are accountable to it.

DIVERGING AND CONVERGING

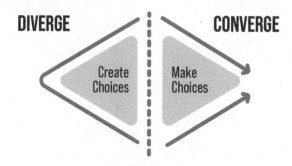

In war gaming, you start with divergent thinking, create choices, and ultimately you converge. This allows for creative thinking and speculation into all the possibilities. Traditional planning is a very linear process to go through. It doesn't encourage diversity of thought and exploration of all the different opportunities that exist.

With traditional planning, leadership starts with assumptions baked in (called *historical context*) and starts planning as if status quo will carry on, undisrupted. Just because leadership is thinking about the marketplace in a particular way doesn't mean that the competition's thinking of it that way, too. Since there is no safe forum for challenging assumptions in traditional planning, leadership ends up carried away by groupthink. Yet they confirm one another's bias and carry on.

War gaming helps leadership to really challenge confirmation bias. Are you asking divergent questions in the right way, with an aim of narrowing down your choices, or are your choices already narrow? And is your perspective from the outside-in, as if from the competition, or is this just internal thinking, based on the status quo?

Are you ready to plan your war game? In the short next chapter, I will walk you through the process of narrowing down your war game to a single core issue.

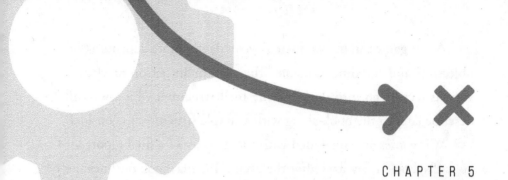

CHAPTER 5

HOW DO I GET STARTED?

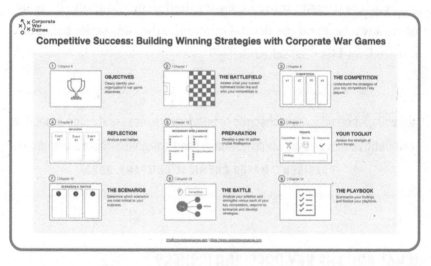

Refer to page 202 in the appendix for a larger diagram.

The war games process can be divided into three distinct phases: planning, conducting, and reporting. Planning for a war game takes place up to three months prior to the event. The pre-gaming phase defines the objectives for the game, identifies the companies that will be represented, prepares a Briefing Book, selects and invites attendees, and determines the logistics for the war game.

A war game can be conducted over a day or more depending on objectives and the time available. They can be in person or virtual; various factors go into deciding the final structure, which we will describe later in the book along with example structures to consider.

War games are concluded with the delivery of a final report, or your Playbook a few days after the event. The Playbook outlines the details of the war game, the insights generated, and the recommendations from the event. This report is circulated to key stakeholders and is used as a guiding document for implementing the proposed actions in business planning that came out of the war game.

Each war game must be customized depending on the issues being addressed and the desired outcomes, the companies being represented, and its final schedule.

We war gamed upcoming changes to our core business and made proactive competitive moves that would not have been possible without a war game.

—PRESIDENT, MAJOR CHEMICAL COMPANY, 2023

WHAT ARE THE KEY PRESSING ISSUES?

The first step in planning a war game is to define the key business issues to address and the core objectives of the game. You can start this process by engaging with stakeholders from different departments to formulate the issues to consider and to determine the level of current understanding on these issues.

This process can be done either by conducting formal interviews with key stakeholders in the business or by a series of informal conversations to ask for suggestions about business issues of concern. A few of these interactions can provide the key business issues that can be the focus of a war game. Involving key stakeholders early in the planning process can help achieve alignment on possible business topics and the objectives of the war game.

TIME FRAME: DO YOU HAVE LONG- OR SHORT-TERM ISSUES?

Your issues can be either long-term/strategic or short-term/tactical. Strategic issues involve changes in your competitive environment, such as regulatory or marketplace. For example, if you're a publicly traded company, you make a lot of statements to the street. You can war game those as well.

If there is a particular competitor that's eating your lunch by winning a lot of different contracts, or you're planning an upcoming product launch, or anticipate a loss of exclusivity, this is an opportunity to tactically war game from a short-term perspective.

Every organization has a business planning cycle. Some companies are annual, while others have a multiyear approach. Integrating war games into the business planning cycle can affect short- and long-term strategic business decisions.

Some companies conduct war games at the beginning of their business planning cycles to take an outside-in approach to planning. Rather than adopting insular business planning, these companies endeavor to understand all the key dynamics affecting their industry. Empowered with this knowledge, they can then develop strategies specific to their business. These strategies are more robust, as they are not created in isolation to what is happening externally.

An alternative approach is to conduct a war game after initial strategies are formulated. This process enables companies to pressure test their strategies against the external dynamics to understand which are more likely to succeed given the competitive reality of their particular industry segments.

Both approaches can be successful. The key is to ensure that a war game is conducted prior to finalizing strategies to ensure that the external dynamics are completely factored into strategic thinking.

WHAT WILL YOU TAKE AWAY FROM WAR GAMING?

As we head into the next part of this book, I'll explain each step in planning your war game. I'd like to give you an overview of what you can expect once you finish your war game:

- You will have a more informed outlook on your industry.

- You will develop a view of how your markets and competitors might evolve and more.

- You will have an understanding of the drivers of that evolution.

- It will be one of the most challenging and stimulating strategic-thinking exercises in your career.

- Most participants walk away with a new capacity for and appreciation of strategic thinking.

- It will provide a way to experience the future together as a company.

- Having lived through the simulation together, participants will have the same assumptions about your competitors, customers, and industry dynamics.

In the next part, we will start working on your Briefing Book. Each part of the process will be explained in a separate chapter. This way, you can refer back to the steps as you get going in the process.

CHAPTER 6

IDENTIFYING YOUR WAR GAME OBJECTIVES

Now we will begin creating your Briefing Book, which you'll use for your war game, distributing copies to each of your teams. The Briefing Book contains information that you'll input by working through each chapter up to chapter 10. At that point, we get into the war game itself.

To start this process, we first need to decide which kind of war game you should play, based on what your objectives may be.

Whether you've got a few competitors or changes, or the other extreme, many competitors or changes, you can war game for any kind of situation. War gaming gives insight into three foundational issues:

1. How to win: When you have a strategy but need to test it.

2. Where to play: When you can see a change on the horizon but aren't sure how to respond.

3. What the game will be: When you have a lot of competitors, disruptions are coming, and you don't know what your operating environment's going to look like.

HOW TO WIN: TACTICAL WAR GAMING

A large paper company back in 2007 was suffering heavy losses. The company brought in a new vice president to turn things around. The VP flew in a few dozen of his top sales leadership to war game a new strategy which he thought would be a sure thing. The home team was assigned his strategy: streamline productivity in order to cut costs and pass the savings on to the customers. They were convinced that their competitors wouldn't have the capability to improve productivity and would lose money if they engaged in a price war by slashing prices.

The other teams, representing the competition, were only told that the large paper company was cutting prices. They responded with a price war and cut their prices, too, because they felt they didn't have a choice. Now all the teams were losing money, including the home team. The VP was dismayed that his strategy was an utter failure. So, he had the participants get creative by brainstorming value adds and exciting promotions. They tested their ideas out and earned more customers. The paper company became profitable.[17]

The VP had come up with what seemed like a sound strategy, but he never rehearsed it. By using a tactical war game, he avoided losses. War gaming is blood and sweat upfront, so you don't have blood and tears later.

---

17 Mark Chussil, "Learning faster than the competition: War games give the advantage," *Journal of Business Strategy* 28, no. 1 (2004): 37–44.

With tactical war gaming, you already know your battlefield, your competitors, and you know what the game is. Now you just need to know, "How do we win?"

WHERE TO PLAY: OPERATIONAL WAR GAMING

Back in 2015, Santander Bank saw the emergence of fintech and cryptocurrency on the horizon. They didn't know how big of a threat these startups would be to their business. In a 2015 *Business Insider* article,[18] Mariano Belinky said, "…this is something we ought to understand. In some cases, it's OK to ignore it and see what happens —in others we should be the first movers and catch this opportunity…." Belinky wasn't sure if Santander should stick its head in the sand or play on a new field.

So, they war gamed fintech startups. The outcome: they should be "the first movers." Santander opened a venture arm and invested heavily in fintech, even purchasing their own tech-based payments-and-banking platform. In 2023, CB Insights published a financial piece[19] on the bank, naming its support of fintech as a core strategy. Santander, it should be noted, is one of Europe's largest multinational banks and has a market cap of $60 billion. Rather than view fintech as a threat, Santander turned it into an opportunity for growth and change.

If you see a threat to your core business, you can war game it to decide whether to stay the course, or pivot.

---

18 Oscar Williams-Grut, "Santander ran war games to see if fintech would kill its business," *Business Insider*, October 20, 2015, https://www.businessinsider.com/santanders-mariano-belinky-on-fintech-war-games-2015-10.

19 Elif Yayla, "Analyzing Santander bank's growth strategy: How the banking giant is investing in fintech," CB Insights Research, March 2023, https://www.cbinsights.com/research/santander-strategy-map-investments-partnerships-acquisitions/.

WHAT THE GAME WILL BE: STRATEGIC WAR GAMING

Your competitors might not even be playing the same game you are. Remember the story of Netflix and Blockbuster from the introduction? Netflix changed the game and Blockbuster just kept on playing their outdated irrelevant game.

Each competitor plays a different game:

If you have uncertainty in your industry, or some other external market event that is likely to disrupt your business, then staging a competitive war game with key players in a safe workshop environment will help you better understand and ultimately react to the changing market dynamics. The aim is to ensure your business isn't surprised or ambushed by any uncertainty. Not just future thinking, but also future practicing prepares your company for the big *what-ifs* that traditional strategic planning frameworks don't account for.

HOW YOU KNOW A WAR GAME IS FOR YOU

Maybe you need to address one or all the issues above in some way, but that doesn't mean a war game is right for you. Not everyone is ready to war game, and I'll talk about that at the end of this chapter. But to know if you're ready, you need to ask yourself these four questions:

1. How confident are you in your current strategy?

2. Can you think strategically and make realistic assumptions?

3. Can you challenge your assumptions?

4. Are you prepared for change?

Smart and talented people are everywhere in our industry. The difference between success and failure sometimes lies in process and tactical execution. Having a rigorous process and dedicating the time and space to truly immerse yourself in the competition's shoes can yield insights, strategies and approaches that might otherwise be missed. Aside from the main objective of the wargaming exercise, another important by-product is closer alignment amongst the teams tasked with driving forward your strategy.

—SENIOR DIRECTOR OF MARKETING, MEDTRONIC

YOU'RE CONFIDENT IN YOUR CURRENT STRATEGY

If you think with 20 percent certainty that your competitor's going to launch a product that will decimate your market share, would you do something about it? How about with 40 percent certainty? Sixty percent? Eighty percent? Risk averse companies wait until near certainty or even until they have historical 100-percent-certain information until they act. And they will fall behind.

I was watching a golf tournament the other day, and the commentators kept talking about this one player who used to be number one in the world, but he wasn't playing well. They would comment, *Oh, that's a good ball, that's going to give him confidence,* and again on another hole, *That's going to give him confidence,* over and over. Although he had been playing shaky in the past, none of that mattered in relation to that day, because with each solid hit his confidence grew toward the next hole and the next, little by little, enabling him to take greater risks, inevitably leading him to a much-needed win.

One of my bosses always used the phrase, "corporate confidence," in terms of our strategy and I thought about that when I was watching the golf game. In golf and in business you can't win unless you have the confidence to bring your *A* game. Otherwise, you'll hesitate to take necessary risks to win. Like the pro golfer, you can be number one in the world at some point, but it doesn't matter because you're only as good as the day that you compete.

If you feel that your company lacks the confidence to take risks and innovate, and you really want to have a culture where it's OK to make mistakes, then make your mistakes and try things out in a war game environment. People will feel better about possibly making the wrong decision because billions of dollars or their jobs aren't at risk. If you aren't sure enough to move forward, war gaming will give you the confidence you need to execute your strategy.

YOU'RE MAKING "REALISTIC" ASSUMPTIONS

Can you think strategically *and* make realistic assumptions? Those two skills are complementary. For strategy, you need to be able to think from a 30,000-foot point of view, or more holistically. This helps you make assumptions based on the overall reality of your industry.

Assumptions can be separated into three categories:

1. Assumptions about your company

2. Assumptions about the competitive environment or the competition

3. Assumptions about the marketplace

All organizations believe their assumptions are realistic, but assumptions can be blind spots, especially if the industry has been static for a while and senior management has been lulled into the complacent, *we've-always-approached-the-business-this-way* bias. And nobody says anything to the contrary. Or, you're all in agreement internally about your assumptions but your competition thinks differently. Maybe they know something that you don't, or it's the other way around. Either way, willingness to challenge assumptions is a critical part of success for gaming.

I think a better question would be the following: Can you think strategically and *challenge* your company's assumptions? Maybe if you're the CEO, this isn't a problem for you. But how often do you see employees challenging *you* or *your* senior management? If the answer is *rarely* or *never*, then war gaming can provide a safe forum for doing just that. The key thing for success is making sure it's not personal and telling everyone, "We're going to have open conversations in this room around our assumptions and what we're thinking about ourselves." If you're ready to do that, then you've got to be ready for the next point.

YOU'RE PREPARED FOR CHANGE

You also need to be prepared to make changes to your plan based on the results of the simulation. That's the difference between an *interesting* versus *actionable* workshop. If you don't get to action, then you've wasted an opportunity to create value. At the end of a war game, you have a Playbook with strategies that all the key players have ideated, tested, and rehearsed. Everyone has the corporate confidence they need to act. The only thing left at that point is to execute.

But willingness to change isn't just a psychological requirement. Timing is everything. When you're at the beginning of a planning cycle, there's a compelling case for doing a war game, but if you're squarely in an executional phase and if you're unable to change anything after doing a war game, it doesn't always make sense.

Some companies, like oil companies, simply can't change direction at a certain point. They invest over $100 million in each well. They scout for oil, invest in infrastructure, then start drilling, and can't switch it off until they've exhausted that source. But the same goes for almost any industry; for instance, if two companies are in a joint venture with a lock-in period of three to ten years, you don't have flexibility to change.

YOU'RE NOT READY FOR A WAR GAME

I've postponed war gaming for companies anywhere from eighteen months to three years because those companies had other priorities. One client was bringing a minimum viable product (MVP) to market. At that point, it didn't make sense to war game. I told them, "You could war game now, but it's going to be a waste of effort and resources, as opposed to when you're a little bit further along in development." Once they tested the probability of success with the MVP, they saw the need for factoring in the competition and war gaming the launch.

In some instances, the issue is internal; for example, a team just isn't ready. They might not be, meaning they aren't talking to each other, or it might be the company has been recently acquired and hasn't yet integrated with their new parent company. For the former problem, war gaming can help with getting teams aligned. But for the latter, they would need to be integrated before they conducted a war game.

I've talked about why you might need a war game, and the answer is *for just about anything*. In the next chapter, I'll show you how to assess the field of battle. In other words, what's happening in your market, and can you war game that?

Refer to page 203 in the appendix for this chapter's template or scan the QR code in the appendix to download a full set of the printable digital templates for this book.

CHAPTER 7

ASSESSING THE FIELD OF BATTLE

W ars are fought with a series of battles, as you can see from the ongoing wars between brands like Coca Cola and Pepsi. Now that you know your war, and you have an overall objective for your war game, it's time to think strategically about where your next battle will be. This is the premise for your war game and the next step in constructing your Briefing Book.

Any given premise may be likely or unlikely, but it's essential that your premise is at least plausible or else the game and the specific scenario on which it is based won't be interesting or credible. Your premise determines what kind of game you're going to play.

SURVEYING THE BATTLEFIELD: TWO KINDS OF RISKS

To determine where your next battle will occur, you can look at two kinds of risks: event risk and trend risk. Event risks are black-swan events, like a global pandemic or an environmental disaster. These are the uncertainties. What are the big changes that might occur in your market should this happen? This is where you use scenarios for your battle, so you can put a plan into place to mitigate risk.

Trend risk is based upon the knowns, or the events that are happening to an industry, in general, e.g., the US population is aging, the demographics are changing. They could be emerging, or they could be currently happening. For this type of war game, you stress test your strategy by war gaming it.

When I conducted the Battle for Home Entertainment for my students at SMU, our Briefing Book mentioned the industry trending toward a more customer-centric approach. This was determined by certain actions: TV players entering the streaming war, like NBC and CNN, improvements in streaming quality, and niche streaming services arising in the market. All these events added up to the customer-centric approach trend. Our teams could then decide if they wanted to war game a strategy for participating in this trend.

REVAMPING CONTENT

- Playing on nostalgia – Content is being re-released from the 80s and 90s to target the millennial population, like *Cobra Kai* based on famous *Karate Kid* on Netflix

- Capitalizing on franchises – Disney acquiring Star Wars and MCU and releasing content around these established franchises

- Facilitating binge watching – All streaming platforms are releasing content week to week and full-season-at-once drops, leading to binge watching

- Focus on original content and docuseries – like documentaries on Ted Bundy and Tiger King

UTILIZING SOCIAL MEDIA	<ul><li>Releasing multiple short videos on social media platforms – Netflix uses YouTube to launch multiple short clips of its stand-up special, which ultimately engages the audience and promotes subscription habits</li><li>Leveraging social media for promotions – Companies like Netflix and Amazon have engaged in multiple social media wars such as quizzes, games and even memes to promote their content and derive user driven content from social media platforms like Instagram and TikTok</li></ul>
CONSUMER CENTRIC APPROACH	<ul><li>Entering niche streaming services – Sony acquired Crunchyroll for around $2 billion, which is a niche anime streaming platform, to increase revenue and subscribers</li><li>Improve in streaming quality – Companies such as Amazon, Apple and Google support a next-gen codec called AV1, which reduces bitrate and increases video streaming quality without the need of higher internet speed</li><li>TV players entering streaming war – NBC launched Peacock in the US in 2020 and Xfinity streaming services were launched by Comcast's Xfinity</li></ul>

The known trends are a good starting point, but what's more critical are the uncertainties, aka event risks. What are the things you don't know will happen? I used to work for a supply chain company with networks around the world, which served the largest retailers in the US. Ten years before the e-commerce boom, one of the key questions that we asked in war gaming was the following: What if we're supplying the dinosaurs? (What if in the future brick-and-mortar retailers no longer have control over their customers who want to buy online?)

In the student war games I teach, we also explore the evolution of industries. One that we're doing currently is the Battle for Home Exercise, which drastically changed due to the COVID-19 pandemic because everyone was at home. Now we're war gaming the new shift back to the gym with the pandemic lockdowns being over. Is every customer going back to the gym or will they continue to work out at home?

These kinds of projections are precursors for scenario planning, which we'll talk about later in the book. When you survey the playing field at this point, you're starting to think through whether you think your industry is going to be business as usual or if there are going to be trends that change it. In terms of these trends that may affect your business, do you want to roll over and play dead and let the competition win or do you want to engage on the battlefield?

EVOLUTION OF INTERNATIONAL CONTENT	<ul><li>According to Netflix, the Spanish series *La Casa de Papel* (*Money Heist*) has been a massive success internationally</li><li>More local-language series are coming up on streaming platforms now. 2020 had 130 new seasons on Netflix alone</li><li>And Amazon is doing the same at a smaller scale</li><li>Prime Video is reportedly producing 17 new original series from the UK, Italy, Germany, Spain, India, Japan, and Mexico</li></ul>
PERSONALIZED CONTENT	<ul><li>Tailored content will be the main driver in the video entertainment industry as it makes content that is specific to each and every individual</li><li>Google TV and Netflix are using AI technologies to provide highly resonant content and personalized recommendations to the customers</li></ul>

IMMERSIVE CONTENT	• Sony is leveraging its "3R Technology"—Reality, Real-time, and Remote—to inspire emotion through the power of entertainment
	• Sony Immersive Music Studios is focused on developing immersive music experiences through the creativity and technology, and is partnering with Sony Music and Verizon to support the development of the immersive experience
	• Going forward, Sony aims to provide new forms of entertainment that visualizes play content and sports data
GAMIFICATION	• Moving forward companies are focusing on gamification as video games or interactive entertainment as a format seems to be the general direction of the storytelling
	• Sony PlayStation comprises Virtual Reality gadgets, which further adds the element of gamification to streaming

Every war game is based on a premise around which the game scenario is built...In the corporate setting, the premise may be the creation of a new business model. Take Apple's iTunes for example; somewhere around the time Metallica began suing Napster over the leak of its "Mission: Impossible II" track in 2000, a light bulb appeared over Steve Jobs' head. Ever the innovator, Apple's CEO saw the peer-to-peer network as more than an illegal nuisance and began to develop a way to leverage the Napster revolution into the next killer Mac app. It has changed the way music is purchased.

—CENTER FOR AMERICAN SECURITY

MAPPING YOUR BATTLEFIELD: KEY INDUSTRY DRIVERS

The key drivers are what's pushing the trends along in any given industry. It's not enough to know what the trends are—you also need to know what is behind the trends so you can anticipate different solutions. For the Battle for Home Entertainment, we narrowed these down to four, based on data points discovered in our research: partnerships and acquisitions, original content development, advanced technologies, and live sports broadcasting. The first key driver, partnerships and acquisitions, answers the *why* behind a trend we saw in the industry: customer-centric approach. Networks were all acquiring or partnering for better services and add-ons in order to attract more customers and add value for loyal customers.

01	PARTNERSHIPS AND ACQUISITIONS

- Video streaming platforms are entering into partnerships and acquisitions to expand their content library, add production capabilities, and expand creative program development

- For instance, Amazon bought MGM, the studio behind the James Bond franchise; Netflix announced a partnership with Excel Entertainment and Amblin Partners, and acquired Night School Studio, a video game developer company; Apple entered a partnership with Playtone, a production company to develop and produce TV content and with Malala Yousafzai to develop dramas, comedies, documentaries, animation, and children's series

02 | ORIGINAL CONTENT DEVELOPMENT

- Companies such as Netflix, Amazon, Apple, Disney, and Sony are investing in developing original content to provide quality content to its subscribers, expanding original content library size and to reduce dependence on production studios for licensing

- Subscription streaming platforms are estimated to invest more than $230 billion in FY 2022, in original content development. Apple, which highly relies on grabbing subscriptions through its original content, is estimated to invest more than $7 billion in content development

03 | ADVANCED TECHNOLOGIES

- Video streaming platforms are leveraging advanced machine learning (ML) to analyse subscribers' viewing habits and preferences. They are also using artificial intelligence (AI) to identify collective behavioural relationships between content that may not be organically related and to make sure platform delivers synchronized user experience across different devices

- Netflix uses ML and AI to identify content viewing habits of its subscribers and to offer related suggestions. Further it uses data sciences to make decisions which could improve the planning of budgets, finding locations, building sets, and scheduling guest actors

04 | LIVE SPORTS BROADCASTING

- Companies are looking at live sports streaming as potentially a key piece of their future success driver for growing the audience of their video streaming services. Major streaming companies are partnering with leagues and broadcasters to gain airing rights

- Apple acquired the broadcasting rights of Major League Soccer from 2023 to 2032. Disney airs live sports streaming of various sports on its application. Amazon has also started live sports on its Amazon Prime application

Going through an exercise like this also helps to align your external market to your internal issues. What's critical for you? How do these key industry drivers affect initiatives you might be planning? How do you address some of these issues?

CNN tried to stream and failed miserably. They spent a lot of time and effort, launched, and within a few weeks the service was gone. They may have benefited from doing a war game, looking at the key drivers in their industry and asking real questions around whether they had the skill sets, capabilities, and resources to go after the shiny new streaming trend, whether they needed to acquire or partner to make up for their deficiencies, or whether they needed to add value for customers in an entirely different way.

What are the key drivers of your industry? And which one do you really want to focus on right now? Where do you want to do your battle? Because you cannot fight every battle all at once. You don't have the resources.

Mars and Hershey's are an example of a more grounded approach. Mars diversified from chocolate and went into other areas liked snacks and pet products, but Hershey's decided, "No, we're just going to stay here in confectionary." Hershey's wanted to compete with Mars, but they also knew they wanted to stick to their core business. Do you stay with your core business, or do you follow your competition? A war game helps you weigh this objectively. A strategy can also be about what not to do.

TAKING INVENTORY BEFORE THE BATTLE: KEY RESOURCES

CNN said, "We're going to get into streaming. We think we have the resources to fight on that battlefield." But they didn't war game it and they died on that battlefield.

Having financial resources is one thing, but having the right skill sets is another. You can throw money at an issue, which is a very military approach, like, "Hey, there's a problem, let's send a battalion of troops and hope that the situation works itself out." But history proves that if you send troops to a battlefield without the right kind of equipment, e.g., desert khakis in Antarctica, it's not going to work. We talk about assessing your resources and your morale to understand if you're going to succeed later in the book, but in choosing the issues you're going to war game, you must at this point think at a high level about internal issues as well.

WEIGH THE ODDS: WHAT'S AT STAKE

To know what's at stake on your battlefield, you must look deeper than the surface. When you look at an iceberg, one tenth of the iceberg is above the water, but then there's the nine-tenths underneath.

Microsoft invested $13 billion in rights to Open AI's ChatGPT AI technology. AI has the power to disrupt the search industry, which is a significant portion of Google's revenue. Google is Microsoft's biggest competitor, and no one's been able to shake Google for twenty years. It wasn't surprising that Microsoft jumped for first-mover advantage, as they knew what's at stake for their competitor is the future of search.

If Microsoft took an inconsequential view of their battlefield, they wouldn't bother with AI, as this isn't their core business. But, if they want to compete with Google, they must disrupt *their* core business, which is search. Nobody has been able to come near to toppling Google in twenty years, but Microsoft is betting on AI being the future of search.

NAME YOUR OPPOSING PLAYERS: EVALUATING THE COMPETITION

In Europe, giant telecoms comparable to American companies like AT&T and Bell used to be operated by their respective governments; one huge entity per country. For example, in the UK they had British Telecom, PTT was the telecom company for Switzerland, Portugal Telecom in Portugal, and so on; all governmental-owned entities. Suddenly, Europe deregulated telecoms, and the market was rapidly flooded with several players. The big telecoms struggled with thinking as competitive entities versus government departments, and they didn't know how to proceed. I worked with Portugal Telecom after the deregulation and the project was around understanding the word *competition* and their new reality. We war gamed to learn how to evolve from a monopoly mindset to a competitive mindset.

Your competitors might be obvious to you, or maybe not. The important thing is that you become aware of *everyone* on the field. Competitive acknowledgment is recognizing your direct *and* indirect competition. Established companies, especially monopolies, struggle with this, as they often have the attitude of "We're on top. We've got market leadership; we don't have any competition. No one can do what we do." This can create blind spots, making them easy prey for indirect competition to take them out of the game, or cause significant losses.

If you're playing a chess game by yourself, you can move wherever you want. But if you're facing an opponent, you need to anticipate their moves. If, with a little competitive acknowledgment, you realize you're up against not just one opponent, but five or six, and that you're not even playing chess but you're playing Chinese checkers, things start to get very complicated.

Keep in mind that from a practical perspective, you can only war game six competitors at the most, because more than that isn't manageable. If your competitive environment is crowded, you'll need to narrow it down by categorizing your competitors; for example, you can look at your direct competitors, new competitors coming into the marketplace, and disruptors.

Your other key players are anyone else who has power in your marketplace. This might be your customers, whom you can rank according to value to your business. If you're not selling a one-dollar widget, but you're selling a ten-million-dollar contract, your customers are important. Many B2B companies war game with the customers in the room, or people who roleplay their customers, asking them: "If we come to you with this value proposition, but our competition comes to you with a different one; which one would you choose?" You can also include suppliers in the room if they're fundamental to your environment, as in certain industries where raw materials are scarce.

Now we know where your battle will be and what you'll be war gaming. But, we can't have a war game unless we have someone to play against. In the next chapter, we'll take a broad look at all the players on the battlefield. You might be surprised by who is there.

Refer to page 204 in the appendix for this chapter's template or scan the QR code in the appendix to download a full set of the printable digital templates for this book.

UNDERSTANDING THE KEY COMPETITORS

I was watching golf the other day, and it occurred to me that business is like golf, in that you don't compete with one team against another, like in soccer or basketball. In golf, just like in business, you compete against yourself, the golf course, the weather, and a myriad of other factors. Your situation, depending on where your ball lies, is different from the other competitors. If you've hit the rough and suddenly you've got a difficult shot, it puts you in a very different position than someone else. Their shots, or strategy, doesn't directly affect you, but their outcomes. Understanding the game is really important, because it gives you context for how you build your strategy and execute.

This feeds into your objective, which we talked about in chapter 6. How broadly you define your war, in terms of many players or just a few, will converge and affect your battlefield. If your battlefield is too narrow with only a few players, you may have blinders on and miss opportunities. If it's too broad, you may not have the right resources to be able to compete.

Michael Porter, in *Competitive Strategy: Techniques for Analyzing Industries and Competitors*, looks at the five competitive forces that can impact your business, which he calls his Five Force Analysis: suppliers, new market players, existing competitors, customers (bargaining power shaping your market), and substitutes.[20]

We talked briefly about enumerating these forces as players on your battlefield in the last chapter, and in this one, we'll take a 360-degree view of everyone who's there. As I mentioned in the last chapter, you might uncover key players that you didn't know existed and this changes the game and or your objective. This is part of that cyclical process.

Understanding your competitors and their perspectives is key to advancing your business forward. Gamifying that understanding drives a deeper mindset into your competitive landscape. Leveraging war games and similar activities are a regular component of our on-going strategic planning process.

–DR. ANNE G. ROBINSON, CHIEF STRATEGY OFFICER, KINAXIS

SIZE UP YOUR EXISTING COMPETITION

Your competitor's toolkit is their capabilities—strengths, weaknesses, and their assumptions. In chapter 10, we go deep into how to gather competitive intelligence (CI) on their capabilities, but, for the purpose

---

20   Michael E. Porter, *Competitive Strategy: Techniques for Analyzing Industries and Competitors* (New York; London: Free Press, 1980).

of this chapter, we'll talk about whether you should even count them among your key players:

- What does the competition think about the market?

- What do they think about themselves?

- And most importantly, what do they think about your company?

One of the questions I ask companies in war games is: *Do you care about your competition?* And even more importantly: *Do they care about you?* I've seen some painful revelations after a few rounds of games with teams representing the competition, where the leadership realizes, "We thought we were the center of the universe in this industry, but these other teams representing our competition didn't even register us as a threat. They were going after other things and their focus was somewhere else." If the competition's not even registering your existence, a war game will help you determine why.

You might be a smaller newcomer to the industry. A C-suite executive for an oil company was referring to his competition when he asked me, "How can a secondhand Chevrolet tell a Maserati what to do?"

Famous last words.

The best strategy for any battle is to respect your competition, even if they're small, because winning isn't about having the most resources; it's about resourcefulness. You can't always win a war by waging a full-on battle, especially when your opponent is waging guerilla warfare. And with the advent of digital marketplaces, templatized marketing strategies, and automated software, suddenly the little guy isn't so little anymore.

UNCOVER NEW COMPETITORS AND OUTSIDE FORCES

Take a look at Zoom versus American Airlines. I don't think American Airlines would have ever counted Zoom among their competition, but as a result of COVID-19, people realized that if the end goal is to have an effective business meeting, they might not need to get an airplane to be face-to-face if they can jump on a Zoom call.

Timelines and regulatory changes can also be emerging players in your battle. Look at California. If the largest state in the US is making zero emission vehicles (electric) mandatory by 2035, then how will Toyota and other car manufacturers make sure a large customer base can charge their cars when the infrastructure and resources won't be there?

Timelines could also be dates. If your competition announces they're going to launch product X in three years, look out.

It could be other sorts of upcoming milestones in the industry, such as changing industry standards, new technology coming to market, new research, and data (especially for the healthcare industry).

The lines of industry are blurring, and you must think about who you're really competing with to understand the key players: traditional and nontraditional alike.

You might not know offhand which competitors are emerging and need to dig deep to make an educated guess. Think about which companies would be interested in your marketplace based on their key characteristics. For instance, if you're in fintech, you might pinpoint a particular niche in your market that any tech company with the right infrastructure, cash on hand, and network could conceivably compete in. Once you get a list of companies who fit these characteristics, you will have a good idea of where new players might emerge.

IDENTIFY YOUR CURRENT AND PROSPECTIVE CUSTOMERS

This exercise can get exhaustive, but it helps to think a little outside the box and look into peripheral industries to see whom your potential customers could be.

Take a lesson from Tim Hortons when it attempted to expand from Canada in the northeastern US in 1984. The restaurant chain took its time, but by 2010 began closing locations, having never gained traction. They failed as they tried to bank on their resounding success in Canada, reusing their same messaging but realizing that Americans didn't care much for what Canadians love. By 2012, they had invested billions of dollars but were making little money from over 800 locations. They began closing operations.[21]

Then with an investment from Burger King, they tried again by opening locations in Houston to much more success. By taking a measured, slow approach, and partnering with local media to appeal to the customer on a personal level, the company plans to expand slowly west until it grows enough market presence to take on Starbucks and Dunkin'.[22]

WHEN COMPETITORS ARE YOUR FRIENDS

Not all players are direct competitors in your market. Take the major airlines, all buying the same jets from the same manufacturers. Often airplane manufacturers won't release a new model unless they have a

21 Samantha Yoder, John K. Visich, and Elzotbek Rustambekov, "Lessons learned from international expansion failures and successes," *Business Horizons* 59, no. 2 (2016): 233–43. https://doi.org/10.1016/j.bushor.2015.11.008.

22 "Tim Hortons hatches plan to build U.S. brand recognition," *QSR Magazine*, n.d., https://www.qsrmagazine.com/exclusives/tim-hortons-hatches-plan-build-us-brand-recognition#:~:text=In%20the%20future%2C%20quickly%20penetrating,restaurants%20will%20debut%20in%202023.

specific number of orders, or it's just not worth it. If two competing airlines both place orders, they inadvertently help each other get what they want. Also think about AT&T and Motorola. They can be competitors, suppliers, and customers of each other depending on the transaction.[23]

Sometimes unlikely cross-marketing partnerships create new opportunities and widen your playing field. Take Mars and Hershey's, when Mars lost the battle for product placement in the film *ET* to Hershey's. Originally, the film producer asked Mars to put their M&M's in the famous scene where ET follows the candy trail left by Elliott. Mars passed, so the producers went to Hershey's, who put their Reese's Pieces in the scene. The deal netted them billions of dollars in sales and put their candy in every concession stand of every movie theater in the country.[24]

TAKE AN OFFENSIVE STANCE

A lack of decision-making and alignment from within an organization prevents that organization from being able to act quickly on opportunities. In chapter 3, we talked about the ten attributes for competitive success, and one was acting quickly when faced with an opportunity.

We go more into assessing your resources in chapter 11, which will help you take a hard look at everything and everyone you have on hand to engage in your battle, but for the purpose of this chapter, start thinking about what your strengths and weaknesses are as a company.

You don't want to be in a position where you're waiting for things to happen in the market, and then you'll act. This is a reactive or

---

23   "The right game: Use game theory to shape strategy," *Long Range Planning* 28, no. 5 (1995): 128. https://doi.org/10.1016/0024-6301(95)90326-7.

24   Simon Vielma, "7 of the worst business decisions in history," Surfky.com., February 16, 2022, https://www.surfky.com/worst-business-decisions.

defensive strategy. From an offensive perspective, if you proactively identify actions that your competition is likely to take, you can pre-emptively strike.

We've been looking externally for the past few chapters. In the next chapter, we start to look within for historical context. You don't want to keep fighting the same battle and getting the same results.

Refer to page 205 in the appendix for this chapter's template or scan the QR code in the appendix to download a full set of the printable digital templates for this book.

CHAPTER 9

ANALYZING PREVIOUS BATTLES

T he business world is constantly changing, but not all companies change their strategies with it. They keep holding on, waiting for what they've been doing to start working again. Instead of reflecting on what happened to them in previous battles, they use the same tactics without any intentionality. Think about the game Rock, Paper, Scissors, where the winning strategy is literally how well you analyze previous battles. The first round is anyone's guess, but you play the next round based on what your opponent previously chose and what you predict they'll do next. Conversely, you wouldn't make the same choice every time, because your opponent will predict your next move and easily counter it. This is why it's important to examine past battles with your competition and make intentional, strategic choices for the future.

Strategy is done in two different parts: formulation, which is future, goal-oriented thinking about where you want to be in the future (*we want to have 40 percent market share by the end of the year*) and execution, which is how you're going to get there (*we increase pro-*

motional activities). A disconnect between formulation and execution indicates that all you really have are ideas. A lot of companies fail because of this, especially startups. You can gauge how well you've been able to execute versus your competition by looking at past battles.

Have you executed your strategy? How did your competition execute?

Look at Walmart versus Amazon, both competing for the same customers, but with completely different assumptions. Walmart was able to analyze their previous battles with Amazon to finally get a win.

Amazon assumed: *People want their stuff sent to their house.*

Walmart's assumption: *Amazon can't do that profitably.*

Amazon persisted, because they had no legacy infrastructure to get in their way, unlike Walmart. They built a global network.

Walmart waited, doing the same thing they always did. They were getting destroyed by Amazon.

Amazon 1, Walmart 0.

Walmart reflected and decided to get into e-commerce to beat Amazon, but Amazon by this time was gaining too much ground for Walmart to enter the market as a newbie. Walmart needed a heavy hitter to help them.

They made a bid for Diapers.com, because they wanted Marc Lore, the e-commerce guru behind the brand, to help them battle Amazon. They lost that battle to Jeff Bezos at Amazon, who saw Diapers.com as a potential competitor and wanted to swallow them by buying them out. He drove the stock down to zero by engaging in a price war and ended up buying the company for pennies. Marc Lore reluctantly went with them for five years, according to the buyout terms.

Amazon 2, Walmart 0.

Marc Lore left Amazon in 2014 to start Jet.com. He wanted to compete with Amazon, whom he openly hated working for.

Walmart reflected on the Diapers.com deal, then came back and acquired Jet.com (and by extension, Marc Lore). After the acquisition, Lore became CEO of Walmart's e-commerce division and turned things around for Walmart.com, making them a serious contender in the e-commerce space. Amazon sold Diapers.com and other sister sites at a loss.[25]

Walmart 1, Amazon 2.

Walmart was doing the same thing over and over and losing, so they thought about it, changed course, and got a win. This is the whole point of reflecting around what worked and what didn't work. When you look at your own past battles, if you were successful, think about ways you could have accelerated your success knowing what you know right now. Also consider ways that you could have mitigated failure if you weren't successful.

When you put this contextual information together, you get a sense of what you can start exploring from a war-gaming perspective. This is a vital part of the preparation for your war game.

The Texas Rangers stadium is filled with cameras and sensors, so they can track every athlete's (home and away) movements as they play and practice. Based on that data, they've built models to calculate the likelihood of each player's success. For instance, when a pitcher throws a ball, the software could measure and predict he will be able to throw 10,000 pitches with accuracy in a season. This number might mean the likelihood of success for him is going to be significantly higher than other pitchers in the league. If the Texas Rangers were to recruit

---

25   Matthew Boyle and Bloomberg, "Walmart head of e-commerce Marc Lore leaving amid the retailer's showdown with Amazon," *Fortune*, January 15, 2021, https://fortune.com/2021/01/15/marc-lore-leaves-walmart-e-commerce/.

him, they would offer him a thirty-million-dollar contract versus a three-million-dollar contract, based on all those numbers and the value he would add to the team.

When you analyze past battles, your process is like how the Texas Rangers measure each player in each game. You gather the data and make informed calculations about future battles based on that data. The difference is you're taking a hard look at yourself.

In fact, this whole process is an act of self-realization.

War gaming is essential to understanding possible future actions your rival(s) may undertake and being able to pressure-test those responses before a decision is made. As a technique, it is an invaluable methodology every company should understand and utilize. War games provide the most impactful benefits when run as a regular program of decision making. It is also important to have stakeholders from multiple parts and functions of the business to bring a holistic view to the situation; often, there are hidden pockets of intelligence within those groups that bring perspective and balance to the exercise.

—JAY NAKAGAWA, DIRECTOR, COMPETITIVE INTELLIGENCE, DELL TECHNOLOGIES

CHALLENGE THE ASSUMPTIONS

When you look at past battles, analyzing and reflecting, avoid making snap decisions about what went wrong or right. If, for example, something didn't work and everyone assumes it's because of x, when really it was x, y, and z, then you're not all seeing the whole picture. You don't want to say, "We're not going to do that again; it didn't work" without picking apart the *why*. You failed because you didn't have the resources, the team wasn't in alignment, you were too late to the market, you used the wrong platform to disseminate this message, your message didn't resonate with the customer, or a combination of all or none of these things.

Timing is also crucial. You might have tried something six years ago and it didn't work out, but that doesn't mean that the same would necessarily hold true today. The competitive environment and ecosystem are always changing and could look very different years later. There's a time and place for innovation, and making sure those different components are in place. Companies struggle with being way ahead of their time, and then they don't go back and try it again because of the risk. You overcome this by laying out the assumptions and asking: What really happened? Why did it happen? What were the conditions that enabled that situation and are things different right now?

REFLECTING BUILDS ORGANIZATIONAL MEMORY

Sometimes companies just don't learn. They'll do a war game and never change and soon forget about everything. Five years later, they're asking the same questions again. They're surprised when they hear that the issue had been addressed. I call this *organizational amnesia*, when you find your company asking the same questions over and over again.

Organizational memory is crucial in combating organizational amnesia, and why the exercise in this chapter is fundamental to your business. If we don't remember past battles, then we all know that history repeats itself.

Look at the news cycle in this country. People go through all kinds of emotions when they hear some news, but a week later, they've forgotten and moved on to the next thing. We repeat our mistakes. The same thing happens with businesses. When you analyze past battles, you activate your organizational memory. When you dig deep and dive back into the history of what's happened in past battles, you build know-how and value.

One of the core advantages of organizational history that established companies enjoy, beyond just the ability to make a product, is their experience and relationships, which take multiple years to build. By reflecting, you're cementing the value of what you experienced.

If you've made products that are successful in the marketplace, you've presumably established suppliers, designers, and other components to help you bring your product to market. As you start running the business, the business to you becomes obvious. But someone new coming in won't have any of that knowledge. It's challenging for them, because they must build that knowledge from scratch. For companies, things that are obvious to them are not obvious to new employees. By reflecting and building your history you also create a healthy culture, where all stakeholders can easily impart the same consistent ideals and lessons to new hires.

As for competitors in the marketplace, part of this is around safeguarding your competitive advantage. You can't protect your trade secrets if you haven't articulated them. One of the large pharmaceutical companies has an estrogen product for women produced from the urine of pregnant horses. But the way that the product is made is a trade secret. It's not even patented. The only reason their competition hasn't been able to come to market with a generic is they've never been able to replicate the company's manufacturing process and they don't have access to the main ingredient.

What is interesting is that the manufacturing process is just a closely guarded secret. This is the power of organizational memory.

DOCUMENT YOUR ORGANIZATIONAL MEMORY

Companies vary in terms of organizational memory. Strategy and direction are well documented for public companies in their guidance and earnings calls. There's some level of accountability from a high stakeholder perspective, but as you go down the organizational hierarchy that diminishes. When you start getting into mid-level decision-making, there's not much accountability, as often middle management is stricken from high-level thinking. When the next generation of middle management leaders comes in, they must start from scratch. How do companies stop starting from scratch? One answer is analyzing past battles and documenting your findings as part of a regular process, making this documentation open to anyone in the company.

When you regularly war game for your strategic planning, you have Playbooks that you can refer to. The key is to reflect and war game new strategies as often as possible. Some companies do it minimum once to twice a year. In fast-moving environments, these companies reflect a lot faster and more often. In more traditional industries, they reflect less often, because they stay static.

DON'T GET TOO COMFORTABLE

One of the most famous rivalries in corporate history is the Coca-Cola versus Pepsi Soda Wars. Up until 1975, it was business as usual for both companies—same Playbooks, nothing new. Then Pepsi came along with "The Pepsi Challenge" and things started heating up, as Pepsi fired a huge shot by claiming their soda tasted better.

Pepsi diversified, purchasing Frito-Lay and other snack food brands. Coca-Cola stayed in beverages, buying energy drinks and other sodas, like TAB. Both changed their labels multiple times, launched targeted marketing campaigns, and made no secrets about their rivalry.[26] What's exciting about the Soda Wars is that neither side ever got comfortable. You can see a mix of long-term plays, where (aside from the New Coke debacle) the brands stayed true to their formulas; and short-term plays, where the brands changed to iconic bottles or cans, revised their logos, or challenged each other in the media. The Soda Wars show how each company analyzes past battles and devises strategies based on historical context.[27]

Repeating your strategy depends on whether you have a longer-term sustainable competitive advantage or a short-term gain. It's understandable that you replicate your core Playbook if you're winning, but also crucial that your Playbook contains a mix of one-off, guerilla-warfare-type tactics that work for outflanking competition by surprise. Back to Rock, Paper, Scissors: if you made the same move every round, your opponent would be ready for it. There's always a tipping point where the field starts to change, and that happens when your competitor can predict what you'll do or when they start behaving differently.

Companies that dominate the marketplace think: *Hey, what we've been doing has been working! There's no need for us to change it.* For this reason, established companies can be resistant to change. If you did something in the past and it worked, that's not necessarily a permission slip to do that same thing again. Ask yourself: Could this happen again? Do the same conditions that were present for success in the

26   Heather Lim, "Coke vs. Pepsi: The history of the age-old cola rivalry," Tasting Table, November 2022, https://www.tastingtable.com/1114104/coke-vs-pepsi-the-history-of-the-age-old-cola-rivalry/.

27   Kim Bhasin, "COKE VS. PEPSI: The amazing story behind the cola wars," *Business Insider*, May 12, 2017, https://www.businessinsider.com/soda-wars-coca-cola-pepsi-history-infographic-2011-11#theyve-both-embraced-the-digital-world-as-social-media-gets-bigger-and-bigger-but-coke-seems-to-be-faring-better-thus-far-17.

past still exist right now? As a rule, if your competitive environment's changing, take note and make changes of your own.

REFLECT ON YOUR VALUE PROPOSITION

You're trying to recognize and learn from your competitive environment while at the same time recognizing that the competition's operations might be different in terms of customers, value proposition, go-to-market strategy, and branding.

A good example of staying true to core values is Hershey's versus Mars in the Chocolate Wars.[28] This was an ongoing rivalry since the turn of the century, beginning with Mars as a customer of Hershey's, to the two taking turns vying for the best-selling candy bar slot over decades, and sprinkled with too many copyright lawsuits brought by either side to recount here. The thing to note is that Milton Hershey was an American icon who built an entire town around his chocolate factory, treating his employees with respect. Stories and legends are still told about Hershey's love for his country and passion for making what he thought was the best chocolate in the world. This value proposition has resonated with Hershey's customers, as the company retains over 40 percent of the chocolate bar market share. Frank Mars didn't build his brand with the same idealized American ethos. The Mars company is known for making popular candy, but it doesn't have the same recognizable brand identity.

An important part of your reflection is around your value proposition versus the competition. Which one holds up better? If you look at most of the brands that have been around for over a century, like Coca-Cola and Hershey's, it's clear to everyone what they stand for,

---

28   Mary A. Yeager and Joel Glenn Brenner, "The emperors of chocolate: Inside the secret world of Hershey and Mars," *The Journal of American History* 86, no. 4 (2000): 1812. https://doi.org/10.2307/2567666.

because their core values haven't significantly changed. How those companies connect with their consumers has evolved over the years, in deference to consumer values, which are always changing. As a company, you must be rigid and adaptive at the same time. Recognize those points of rigidity: which are non-negotiable versus those you must be willing to change with.

REFLECT ON YOUR CUSTOMERS

For this exercise, you might reflect externally, internally or both.

- External reflection: In your previous battles, who connected with your customers more effectively? Could you have helped your customers gain satisfaction or a solution better than the competition?

- Internal reflection: If you failed your customer in some way, or proved successful, was this due to internal operations rather than comparing yourself to the competition? Maybe your customer service lines are horrible, there was no follow-through, or you didn't have the right answer.

Two companies in the same marketplace might speak for their customers very differently, like McDonald's versus Burger King. Burger King has been fighting a one-sided war against McDonald's for decades, spending billions on marketing efforts and switching ad agencies multiple times to fight for that elusive number one fast-food-chain spot, while McDonald's has stayed true to their core customers and branding, hasn't changed much in the way of marketing and has steadily expanded across the world, holding steady at number one. It wasn't until this past decade that Burger King emerged with a consistent brand identity that resonated with their customers.[29]

Remember what happened to Toys"R"Us: They had to liquidate all their 700 plus stores because they just didn't realize that the loyalty in their customer base was shifting. Sears was an early pioneer of the catalog business in the US, but they struggled for decades because they didn't reflect on how to create value for their changing customers. Home improvement stores like Lowe's and Home Depot went through struggles as well, because they started oversaturating the marketplace to such a large degree that they suddenly had stores right across the street from each other.

BE INTENTIONAL IN YOUR REFLECTION

The worst thing companies can do in decision-making is to throw things at the wall and hope something sticks. Looking at past battles helps mitigate this strategy, or lack thereof, because it forces you to pause and not react. A lot of times companies just go with the flow, like rudderless boats on a river with no control over their direction. And it shows.

Bed Bath & Beyond, to save itself, threw so many conflicting strategies at the wall that it confused its customers, worried its suppliers, and ultimately disappointed its investors. In 2018, Bed Bath & Beyond was a huge retailer with more than 1,500 stores. But with each failure (e-commerce, private label, stock buybacks, replacing key leaders), they failed to reflect on why they lost past battles. In a panic, they threw ideas out and jumped on them, unsurprisingly getting deeper into debt and alienating their customers. Bed Bath & Beyond

---

29   Chris Kelly, "Burger wars: How Burger King's rivalry with McDonald's reverberates through adland," Marketing Dive, May 17, 2022, https://www.marketingdive.com/news/mcdonalds-burger-king-brand-rivalry-burger-wars/621713/.

didn't have a problem with execution, but they did have a problem with intention.[30]

Part of your reflection is around making sure that you deliberately think about what direction you took and why. Were you intentional in your decision-making or could you have put more thought into it?

Another part to this is if someone on your executive team, or you, threw out a not-so-smart idea, did anyone below you challenge that with a productive conversation? Your company culture must support and encourage conversations where someone two pay grades below you can say, "Hey, you know what? Your strategy didn't work last time." Because none of this is personal.

REFLECT ON WHAT OTHER COMPANIES DID

If you're asking a question in the world of business, you're probably not the only person who's asked the same thing. Others have thought it through and might be at more advanced stages in tackling those same kinds of issues. Think beyond the geographical or product scope of your company. Startups in Chile have asked me questions very similar to those asked by companies in Dubai or in South Africa. Piggyback on that learning and accelerate your knowledge.

At this stage, you've done your reflection on past battles and have begun identifying where your gaps might be. The key to building solid strategies now is basing them on data. It's time to go out and do some research, so that you have the right inputs to craft your strategy. Competitive intelligence plays a large part in this. For the next chapter, we dive deep into your competition. You'll be shocked at how much information is out there.

---

30 "Bed Bath & the great Beyond: How the home goods giant went bankrupt," NPR, April 24, 2023, https://www.npr.org/2023/04/24/1152070914/bed-bath-the-great-beyond-how-the-home-goods-giant-went-bankrupt.

Refer to page 206 in the appendix for this chapter's template or scan the QR code in the appendix to download a full set of the printable digital templates for this book.

CHAPTER 10

GATHERING INTELLIGENCE

F or the final chapter in creating your Briefing Book, we'll do a deep dive into the competition, or what I call a *competitive x-ray*. This is where you look behind the surface, or under the competition's skin to understand the bones of their operation. Remember to include more than just your existing competition, but also the emerging entities and indirect competitors that we teased out in chapter 8, in order to think about how they all will be attacking you.

In 2012 Endo Pharmaceuticals (a company I used to work for), maker of a topical analgesic approved for arthritis called *Voltaren Gel*, released their corporate guidance, which reported an expected upside of more than $200 million for extra years of product exclusivity.

A Goldman Sachs analyst asked caught this and said, "Hold on a second. I believe you said you expect exclusivity through at least 2013. Correct me if my notes are wrong, but I think that points to a longer exclusivity than you previously pointed to."

The COO responded, citing our competitive intelligence. We had done some primary research and got data points indicating that our competitor, which we had assumed was much further along in clinical development to bring out a generic, was, in fact, not. They were still in clinical trials. We got our information through primary research, where we understood they were still in development.

Over the next year, the company went through significant changes, hired new leadership, got rid of commercial functions and other vital departments. They decided, "We're not going to do CI, we're not going to do research. It's a waste of money and resources. We can allocate resources somewhere else, and it'll be more productive."

In 2016, they released their guidance again, saying they didn't expect a generic to come to market. Three weeks later, a generic was approved by the FDA. On March 21, the day that the generic was approved, they gave a statement vaguely reporting that they were evaluating several options regarding this and would provide additional details regarding the potential.

Their stock price went down 3 percent. That's 3 percent of $10 billion. The 2015 product sales were $207 million. When you look at impact, that's a $300 million reduction in the market value of the company.

When a generic launches in the pharmaceutical market, the branded product loses 60 percent of revenue, just as a rule of thumb. For Endo, that's a $124 million downside. All combined, Endo took a $424 million hit. The lesson: spending a little bit of money and time on competitive intelligence to know what's going on in your market is clearly worth it, because no company wants to end up in a situation like this.

The critical piece to competitive intelligence is how you piece together the information. A few years ago, we were war gaming with a vaccine manufacturer. This company had several vaccine manufacturing facilities around the world, so they knew how many vaccines they could potentially supply each country.

The war-gaming scenario was if the company hard negotiates with a government, and one of their competitors comes in, undercuts them and says, "OK, you need 500 million doses. The company's offering it to you for five dollars a dose; we'll give it to you for two dollars." The key question was the following: "Can our competition produce at the scale that we can or not?"

As part of the intelligence gathering, we mapped out all the vaccine manufacturing facilities in the world, so that we could potentially enter a government negotiation and promise the supply they needed and not be undercut by the competition.

We started with Belgium, because a lot of the world's vaccine production occurs there. It was the second largest producer of vaccines in the world. In Belgium, as in many European countries, if you go into the local fire department, they'll give you access to the blueprints for manufacturing facilities. We looked at the blueprints for the competition's vaccine manufacturing facilities in Belgium and determined where the machines were and their sizes. We could equate how many liters of vaccine each facility could produce, for example, one could make 800 liters, another 1,000, and so on. We broke that down into number of doses per company.

We found, for example, one company could make 400 million doses in their facilities. Another company could manufacture 200 million, and the third company could produce 100 million. Then we found out that the company that could make five billion doses was already tied up in contracts they already have, to the tune of 90 percent of the production. We did this for all the other competitors, as well.

From there, it was simple math to find out what our leverage points were.

With competitive intelligence, you must dig deeper. The biggest hurdles are not knowing how to do the research[31] and laziness.

BE SHERLOCK HOLMES, NOT JAMES BOND

When I mention competitive intelligence, the first thing a lot of people ask is, "Is it espionage? Like corporate spy stuff?"

I tell them, "No, it's not about being James Bond, where you steal information. It's more like Sherlock Holmes, where you look for clues and put them together, like pieces of a puzzle."

As a cautionary tale, I tell my students about the P&G, Unilever espionage case,[32] where P&G offered to pay Unilever $10 million. P&G had hired a CI agency to collect information about Unilever, their competition. The agency went through the trash at Unilever and found sensitive documents. While this wasn't against the law, it was against P&G's ethics policies. When the P&G lawyers saw the agency's report, they said, "Oh no, this is trouble." They immediately gave the documents back to Unilever, promised not to use the contents to gain an advantage, and paid them $10 million. P&G also fired three people linked to hiring the agency.

This is why it's important to do the research legally and ethically. Corporate espionage is illegal in the US and in many parts of the world. Use this three-part rule to be your guide:

---

31 For a deeper dive, refer to Mike Ratcliffe and Arjan Singh, *Best Practices in Managing Competitive Intelligence Research: For Pharmaceutical and Biotechnology Managers* (CreateSpace Independent Publishing Platform, 2016).

32 Julian E. Barnes, "P.& G. said to agree to pay unilever $10 million in spying case," *The New York Times*, September 7, 2001, https://www.nytimes.com/2001/09/07/business/p-g-said-to-agree-to-pay-unilever-10-million-in-spying-case.html.

1. Don't misrepresent yourself

2. Don't steal information

3. Don't lie to get information

GATHERING INTELLIGENCE AS A PROCESS: QUICK OVERVIEW

The first question you ask your team is, what are we interested in, whether it's an established competitor, emerging competitors, or other entities? Is our interest longer or shorter term?

The second question you ask is the following: What do we need to know about them? What information is crucial?

Now you source map in three steps:

1. Open sources. This is where search engines, like Google, are a great starting point. But you don't stop there at the easily available information.

2. Primary research. You need to think outside the box, here. Follow the flow of information.

3. Put the story together with multiple data sets. The most valuable, and the most complicated part.

TACTICAL VERSUS STRATEGIC COMPETITIVE INTELLIGENCE

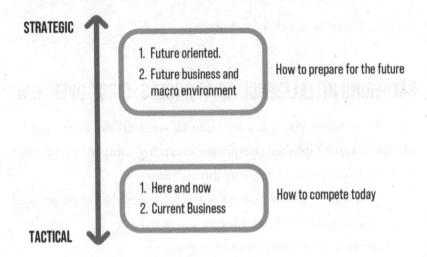

STRATEGIC

1. Future oriented.
2. Future business and macro environment

How to prepare for the future

1. Here and now
2. Current Business

How to compete today

TACTICAL

Back to that first question for your team: Are our interests longer or shorter term? This is the difference between tactical and strategic intelligence.

Tactical intelligence answers questions such as the following: What are we selling? Whom are we selling it to? How is the competition going to attack us? How do we compete today? What's the competition's product? What's their price? How are they promoting it? What's their distribution? It's about here-and-now business for the short term. Sales and marketing rely heavily on tactical intelligence.

Strategic intelligence is much more future oriented and answers questions such as the following: What will the macro environment look like, and how do we prepare for the future? What are the core dynamics of the industry? How is the industry changing? How is the operating environment changing?

Let's say you have a big competitor in the marketplace that you know has large cash reserves. They've signaled an intent that they're going to grow significantly to increase their market share. You know that at this point, they don't have the capability to do that quickly unless they acquire an existing organization. Your strategic intelligence would answer the question: Who are they going to acquire? So, you start gathering intelligence to find out.

Which type of intelligence you gather depends on your company's time horizon. For example, strategic for a tech company is much shorter than an oil and gas company, usually one year versus twenty years.

INTERESTING VERSUS ACTIONABLE INTELLIGENCE

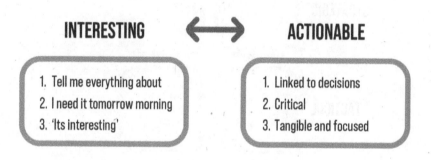

INTERESTING ⟷ **ACTIONABLE**

INTERESTING	ACTIONABLE
1. Tell me everything about	1. Linked to decisions
2. I need it tomorrow morning	2. Critical
3. 'Its interesting'	3. Tangible and focused

Now for the second question you ask your team: What information is crucial? This is the difference between interesting and actionable intelligence.

Determining whether intelligence is just interesting or actionable is where the filtration comes in. If you asked your team, "Tell me everything about this company, and I need to know it by tomorrow morning." They might push back and say, "Why do you really need answers to everything, now?" Rather than waste resources on interesting facts or stories, whittle this down to the critical things that you do need.

Actionable intelligence is linked to decisions. It's tangible and focused. For example, if you want to sell a product to a niche customer, you probably don't need to know everything about your competition. You can start with what their strategy is in that segment, and what they've done historically. If they've got unrelated businesses, you don't really need to know about them.

When I ask companies to start thinking about their intelligence requirements, I segment this into four boxes to help them organize their thoughts. There's strategic and tactical, interesting, and actionable. Where they all should be focusing on is the upper right-hand side, where your needs are strategic and actionable.

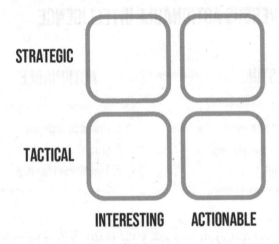

OPEN-SOURCE INTELLIGENCE GATHERING

When I teach war gaming at SMU, I often conduct small experiments to prove a point. For one class, I gave the two teams information that had been gathered from a Google search and told them both to analyze the same company.

And guess what happened?

Both the teams came up with the exact same analysis.

Google does not have all the answers. Google tends to be the starting point for people, which is great, but the trouble arises when it's the single source of truth. The issue with Google or any search engine is there's zero competitive advantage. The information you find on the internet happens to be the same information everyone has access to. It's the same with emerging generative AI tools.

And you'll be surprised how much of that there is. Publicly traded companies release a surprising amount of information online, like quarterly filings, investor decks, and annual statements, called 10K filings, that they are required to submit to the Securities and Exchange Commission (SEC). These statements contain all their assumptions.

Private companies generally release a lot less information, but you can still find clues in press releases, trade shows they attend, podcasts, blogs, social media, and other marketing copy. From there, you can gain an understanding of how they're thinking about the market.

For private and public companies, you can also try patent analysis, which you can look up on the United States Patent and Trade Office (USPTO) website or find global patents in your search. If a competitor files for patents or intellectual property this can give you great intelligence about where they're heading. But, being open source, this is a common technique. Some companies will not publish patents because, as soon as they're published, they become public and they see a whole series of copycats from different parts of the world producing the same thing, where they may not have protections. Coca-Cola and KFC, for example, never patented their secret recipes.

PRIMARY RESEARCH: FOLLOWING THE FLOW

Competitive intelligence is the notion of going beyond the obvious. It's around providing actionable intelligence to support decision-making. In the context of a war game, you ask questions and define your needs based on what your organization requires, versus thinking about what resources you think are available. Because you'd be very surprised about the information you can find if you know where to look.

At this point, you move beyond easily available, open-source information and get closer to what's likely to happen in the future. This is where primary research comes in. You can find primary source information by following the flow. Start with who produces the information, then move to where it's collected, find out where it's transmitted, and look at other people that have interest in that information.

Government bodies accumulate a lot of information that the public has access to. For example, the Sunshine Act in the US has to do with pharmaceutical companies, who are notorious for spending a lot of money on physicians—vacations, dinners, gifts—to get them to prescribe their products to patients. The Sunshine Act requires pharmaceutical companies to publicly disclose all payments or gifts to physicians over a small amount. If you wanted to learn who the top doctors your competition engages with are, you could find that information on a US government website.

I conducted a war game for a major airline who wanted to determine the future of transatlantic travel. Traditional airlines used to have four class configurations: economy, premium economy, business, and first class. Then the US carriers started compressing first class and business together, because not many people bought $10,000 tickets. One of the key competitors for the war-gaming client was British Airways. The client was about to order new airplanes and didn't want to configure them until they knew what British Airways' strategy would be on their JFK to London route, which was very profitable for them, as they had a near monopoly with landing slots in both airports. That information, of course, wouldn't be publicly available anywhere, ordinarily.

After an online search, we found something that might help, but we couldn't get access to it unless we were in person. So, we visited the Greenwich University library in London and searched their directory for case studies, which happened to also contain business school graduate students' theses. One student had spent the whole summer doing an internship with British Airways. The title of the thesis was *British Airways Long Haul Strategy.* There it was. An eighty-page document publicly available and it contained everything we needed to know.

One more caveat. When you get into primary research, it hasn't been published, so it's not vetted for you. You must filter the information, because a lot of times it's incorrect. You don't want to make million-dollar decisions based on potentially fictional information. You can rate the source's reliability in terms of high, medium, or low. This gives key stakeholders a guideline on how much credence to give a piece of information. I caution you because I've seen people put an unconfirmed rumor on a slide and the entire room takes it at face value, only to have that information prove wrong and cost them.

PUTTING THE PIECES TOGETHER BY USING MULTIPLE DATA SETS

Creatively identifying and using multiple data sets are critical to help you create and build a "complete" picture of what's really going on. I worked for a pharmaceutical company with a billion-dollar patented product facing a generic threat from a competitor. One of the key questions that came out that we were going to war game was whether it was real or just noise. The competitor had been publicly saying, "We're going to launch a product which is going to eat into your billion-dollar product. And we're going to launch it quickly."

I had independent research teams look at the issue and tackle it from multiple data points. Each team did not know that other teams existed. The teams looked at manufacturing facilities. Some teams reviewed local permits and others looked at blueprints. They figured out capacity. And who could manufacture the machines needed to increase production. They looked at access to raw materials. I got all these data points from different places indicating the same thing: the competitor could not produce enough generic to go to market. They were bluffing.

Sometimes using data sets is easy if the data is clean to begin with. Cushing, Oklahoma, is known as the oil crossroads of the US, because most of the major oil pipelines flow right through there. That's an immense amount of oil coming as far north as Canada, as well as east to west. This tiny town in the middle of nowhere is a huge determinant of oil prices in the world.

There are major consultancies that rent offices in Cushing and run lasers right through the windows into the pipelines to measure oil flow on a real-time basis. That data is transmitted to commodities traders in New York City and in the Mercantile Exchange in Chicago, who do real-time trading based on the flow of oil through Cushing, Oklahoma. But anyone can buy a subscription.

Another source of data not as clean as the above example is incoming freight to US ports. This is customs data available to the public. If you go on the Customs and Border Patrol (CBP) website, the dirty data is available, but it's unreadable. Third parties extract the data, clean it, and present it visually. This is helpful if you want to know who your competitors' suppliers are. The clean data will show you their suppliers, where they receive shipments from, how often, the quantities, and the factories of origin.

If, for example, you wanted to track a mobile phone company to see how many phones they want to sell, you can map out their supply chain. Most cell phones are made in China and get shipped to Shanghai, which ships to Long Beach. The US customs data will show you the number of containers coming into the US for that mobile phone company. Based on the size of the phone, you can figure out how many fit into a carton, then how many cartons fit into a container; multiply by the number of containers and you have a data point approximating the number of phones coming into the US. This gives you an idea of that company's sales predictions.

Most of the time you must put the pieces together yourself. We were war gaming for a company who wanted to find out which company their competitor was going to acquire next. We had all these marketplace signals, found through open-source information (press releases and whatnot) that an acquisition was coming, and it would change the battlefield.

The open-source information was coming from corporate, so we decided to follow the primary source, being the CEO, knowing that he would lead us to the company to be acquired as he would be in negotiations with them. Before you say that sounds more like James Bond than Sherlock Holmes, let me explain. This was a two-step process.

In the US at this time, it took about thirty seconds to find out where almost any private jet was going or had been. Every single plane in the US is registered on Faa.gov (Federal Aviation Administration website) in a searchable database, where you can look up a company and see what plane or planes they own. Every jet is assigned what's called a *tail number*. We looked up the competitor, saw they had one private jet, and wrote down the tail number.

Using an app called FlightTracker.com, we put in the tail number and were able to track their jet's movements. (Now people can switch that tracking off, but at this time that wasn't an option.) We read the log to see where the CEO was flying. We saw that the plane landed in a very small airfield in a tiny city with only one major company's headquarters. From there, it wasn't hard at that point to deduce whom the competition was acquiring.

None of this information was available through Google. But we didn't steal it, either.

Congratulations! At this point, your Briefing Book is complete. Your Briefing Book should have two sections: (1) information on the market and (2) information on each of the companies in the battle's value chain (the x-ray into an organization).

You're ready to start your first war game. In the next chapter, we start by looking at your toolkit. What are you bringing into your battle?

Refer to page 207 in the appendix for this chapter's template or scan the QR code in the appendix to download a full set of the printable digital templates for this book.

CHAPTER 11

ASSESSING TROOP STRENGTH, MORALE, AND RESOURCES

The telecommunications industry, when telecom was exclusive to land lines, had a robust infrastructure and engineers with many years of experience. Then the internet came along, and traditional telephony began to move to IP, or internet protocol, which was based on giant servers. They went from a linear network to a distributed network. The skill sets required to compete in IP telephony were different from telecommunications, which is why a lot of these traditional carriers struggled. They didn't have the skill sets to evolve.

At the time of this massive shift, I worked in an office in London. British Telecom, the number one telecommunications provider in the UK, sold our office a next-generation PBX. They said, "We'll give you this new one with IP telephony. It gives you all these great features you can't get in a traditional telephone box, like voicemail on your computer."

We said, "Great, we'll buy it," and were one of their first customers to make the shift.

British Telecom sent their lead engineer over to install it in the office. His name was Darren, and he was in our office troubleshooting every single day for the next six weeks. So, we gave him his own desk and he became a part of our office. Although he had been somewhat trained on the next-generation IP telephony boxes, we soon realized nobody in his entire company had the skill set to compete in the new IP telephony world.

In this instance, if British Telecom were to have war gamed a shift to internet IP telephony, they would have understood their weakness in terms of skill sets. Then they'd have to figure out two things: (1) How do we bridge the gap between what's needed to compete? (2) What resources do we have right now? A lot of times, established companies will ignore situations like this, as did British Telecom. They wouldn't acknowledge that they had a deficiency, but proceeded anyway.

In creating your Briefing Book, you've also learned that your competitors all have different capabilities. Winning your war game and in fact your market depends on who best uses the resources they have. I call these resources *toolkits*.

At this point, you're about to move into your war game and will need to think about what resources you have at your disposal. Resources are straightforward: capital, capabilities, infrastructure, or a combination of these three.

The softer part of your resources is fundamental to your war game: Do you have the morale to execute on your strategy? This chapter will help you get an objective understanding of your current situation going into your first battle, because nobody wants to walk into a situation in which they're going to get slaughtered.

Let's look at your own toolkit to prepare for your battle.

TIME TO GET OUT YOUR TOOLKIT

When my students played The Battle for Travelers, we had six different teams: major airlines such as American and Delta, overnight stay companies such as Marriott Corporation and Airbnb, and finally online travel agencies (OTAs) such as Tripadvisor, Expedia, and Booking.com.

Each market player was trying to control the traveler in different ways according to their capabilities, or toolkits—in other words, same goal, different parts of the industry. Marriott, for example, wants the traveler to book on their websites, not through third parties. Marriott's capabilities are its trusted, diverse brand offering multiple price points, and ubiquity, like Starbucks, in that they're everywhere. They offer travelers additional benefits in order to circumvent paying commissions to OTAs. The OTAs are trying to control the traveler with discounts and loyalty programs. The airlines, like American Airways, are competing similarly to the overnight stay companies: Don't book through third parties, book straight through us, and use our credit cards to get miles. American Airways attracts travelers with multiple, direct routes. All six companies from the travel industry are competing for the customer, with distinctive offerings.

The scenario that we played was the following: What if there was consolidation in the industry, e.g., if United Airlines, Amex Travel, Hilton Corporation, and Amadeus Travel combined to form the first truly integrated travel company in the world? With this scenario, the industry suddenly shifted from all these players competing in slightly different parts of the industry, to competing against one company possessing all their capabilities. The sum of the parts completely changed the game.

For this game, we invited the American Airlines Head of Commercial Planning, and the Hotels.com Head of Branding to be judges. When we introduced the scenario to them, at first, we were met with shocked silence. After a beat or two, they both agreed that they could anticipate this happening in their industry, and it would profoundly change the competitive dynamics therein. Through our war game, they were able to examine their own resources, or core competencies, and that of their competitors played out on the teams.

Your capabilities are the toolkit of your organization. Your toolkit differentiates you in terms of how you use the same raw materials your competition has access to in novel ways.

We have many ways to look at capabilities, but here are a few to get you thinking:

- SWOT analysis: strengths, weaknesses, opportunities, and threats.

- Four corners analysis: What is a company currently capable of, what are they currently thinking and doing, and what are they likely to do in the future?

- Value chain analysis: How your company creates value and understanding the core components of that.

- Business model canvas: What your core value proposition is, how you go to market, connect with customers, and run operations in terms of your systems and processes.

For the purpose of your first battle, you'll go to your Briefing Book and examine the skill sets you have in your company, the relationships that you've built up, and your reputation in the industry. You'll get an overall sense of how the company you're representing looks at the world, and how your competition does the same. Once you put all of the above together, the goal in the game is to find ways to create unique value for your customers that your competition can't replicate.

TAKING INVENTORY OF YOUR TOOLKIT

You can break your resources down into five categories:

1. Financial (how much capital on hand)

2. Physical (retail locations, warehouses, and equipment)

3. Intellectual (patents and trademarks)

4. Human (troops, morale, and skill sets)

5. Digital (technology, data, and underlying infrastructure)

When you formulate your winning aspiration for your game, you can look at your toolkit and say to your team, "We want to be number one in the world in this particular area. That's a great aspiration. Do we have the resources that it'll take to be able to do that?"

Starting at number one, you take stock, "Do we have the finances for advertising and building relationships?"

If the answer is no, rather than say, "Our aspiration is likely to fail because we don't have this resource," you change this to another question: "Given what we have, how do we maximize it?" And you move down the line, continuing to take stock.

Challenger brands, or scrappier market disruptors, recognize new opportunities in the marketplace and act on them with any resources they have on hand and are ultimately successful. Corporate giants usually don't see it coming.

T-Mobile is a great example. When they came into the market, they went up against Verizon, AT&T, and Sprint with the worst network in the US. Their coverage quality was bad, their customer service was poor, and their scale was much smaller than the big players. When they recognized that they didn't have the same resources as their competition, they changed the market. They did a really good job by maximizing their marketing skill set, branding themselves as the "uncarrier" and doing away with contracts. They offered a far better deal than the other carriers with unheard-of add-ons, like unlimited data, and free international roaming. They also partnered with other large brands, such as Taco Bell, AMC Theaters, and Shell, to offer freebies and deep discounts to customers in their T-Mobile Tuesdays app. They more than doubled their market share as a result.

LINE UP AND SURVEY YOUR TROOPS

Is your team capable or incapable of doing this war game?

Going into any battle, you're going to have weaknesses and strengths. Your challenge is to figure out how this informs your strategy. If you spot a weakness, for instance, if you're lacking in troop strength or skill sets in certain areas, get scrappy and find the resources you need, because the real battle for the market will occur, with or without you. A war game provides a safe environment to have this conversation.

My company had once done a war game for one of the largest financial services companies in the US. When we were looking at the team composition, we noticed that the players were all from upper management. In allocating staff for the teams, they decided they didn't want their direct reports in the room. They kept the war game only to senior management, because, as they explained, "We're going to have some very honest and harsh conversations around our capabilities, or lack thereof, that we don't want the rest of the organization to know about until we build a solution."

When the business model in your industry starts changing, you need to have the skill sets within your company to be able to adjust. Sometimes a war game will reveal the need for transformational changes in your organization. It's a chance for your leadership to align and devise a plan, before you communicate with the rest of the organization. In this stage, you'll want to look at the skill sets you have among your generals, or key stakeholders. If you come up short, back up and war game your leadership team, because you can't fight a battle without talented generals.

For example, I run war games for pharmaceutical companies quite often. For one company, the scenario was around traditional pharmaceutical companies going beyond just selling products. The future, they had decided, was wholistic healthcare with end-to-end services. Pharma companies are typically straightforward: They discover a potential product, go through human testing, get it approved by the FDA and bring it to market. When they suddenly layered in services on top of that, the approval and reimbursement processes added complications they didn't have the skill set to meet. The company's leadership team was used to selling products. In this instance, the issue came out in the pre-battle stage—they needed to get their leadership together to even begin to compete.

GET A FEEL FOR OVERALL COMPANY MORALE

Having great resources and skill sets is only part of what you need for your battle. If you don't have the *support* to be able to execute, then you're likely to set yourself up for failure. Making sure that your troops and generals are motivated and believe in the strategy is the most important weapon in your toolkit.

I don't think there's ever been an instance where prior to a game, a tennis player refused to play because their morale was low. But it quickly becomes apparent during the game when morale is an issue for a player, making it impossible for them to win. Morale, or confidence, is directly correlated with capabilities. Most athletes tend to be realistic in terms of what level of play they can engage in based on their skill levels. For instance, if you're a tennis player and you know you'll never go to Wimbledon, you could still compete on any number of different levels to win in your niche. Similarly, most companies should make realistic goals based on their capabilities (and, of course, stretch themselves a little, just like athletes) because competing at a level you aren't at all equipped for is demoralizing and self-sabotaging.

Here's the surprising thing: For your company to win in a marketplace, you don't need to have the best products, but morale is imperative. Look at some of the previous Microsoft operating systems. Everyone, including the employees, knew they were substandard. Because of Microsoft's marketing strength, distribution, and relationships with resellers and computer manufacturers, they've succeeded. These skill sets gave them high enough morale to stay competitive in the marketplace.

Continuing with business as usual is easy. It's a lot harder to change either the structure of your business or even more difficult, the structure of your marketplace. Winning a battle like this comes from a challenger mentality endemic to the entire organization. Salesforce is a great example of strong, cohesive morale. Salesforce came into the CRM world with an entirely novel, unique value proposition to put their software on the cloud, versus an Oracle or Microsoft Dynamics on-premises installation. Salesforce's Marc Benioff and his team asserted that they would change the world of computing to a cloud-based, Software-as-a-Service, subscription-based model. It was a dynamic shift that no one else was willing to make a bet on. But Benioff built his team around very different skill sets than what Oracle or the others had, and they all shared the same enthusiasm for changing the entire industry.

Morale is the difference between connected and disconnected employees. Connected employees are motivated. They're in alignment with company values. That comes from communication, feedback, and meaning in their work. High-morale environments meet that hierarchy of needs.

Low morale environments are caused by a lot of pivoting in the work being done. People work on projects, and suddenly they're discarded. There's a stark lack of alignment in terms of value. The company leadership says one thing, and then does something else. How many times has your company pivoted from a proposed plan? Or, if you've been talking about a goal for the last five years, have you executed anything to move forward, or has your leadership team just generated more talking points around it?

I once ran a joint-venture game for two different pharmaceutical companies. I'd been warned about a lot of issues with the development of their product, but it still had a lot of potential to be a multi-billion-dollar venture. The setbacks, from what I understood, were mainly cultural issues. I was warned that I wasn't going to be walking into a happy environment in this workshop.

We designed the core objective around making their product a success. In the war game, we encouraged exploration of different strategies that they hadn't thought about, adding robust elements of innovation and brainstorming with a common goal. It worked well. They came out of the war game with a strategy that they tweaked a little, and the resulting morale was much higher, because everyone in the room was aligned on what their next steps would look like. They'd already thought through how the competition was going to attack and they felt ready.

On multiple occasions where morale may be low, war gaming gives your team the corporate confidence to look through all the different options and maximize what's at your disposal. Part of this goes back to winning. Winning is about building a solution aligned to what you have and what you don't have. Recognizing a path toward a solution everyone builds together helps with morale.

CERTAIN PLAYERS EFFECT MORALE

As you organize your teams, you want to balance negative personalities with more positive types. In a previous chapter, I mentioned that often leadership will observe a war game to identify the top performers in their organization. Conversely, morale issues caused by certain personality types quickly become apparent.

War games will highlight internal problems like negative employees, and not having alignment in the organization whether it's a simple issue, for example, differing definitions of the marketplace, or it's more complicated and the misalignment is cultural. Most US companies tend to be more collaborative than other countries, with looser hierarchical structures. Compare this to Asia, where morale tends to be very different by design, due to strict hierarchies.

I once ran a war game for a large mobile phone manufacturer in Asia that couldn't agree on anything. Their strategic planning department was globally responsible for the success of their mobile phones. During the first five minutes of the workshop, we showed a slide with a very simple definition. They debated that one slide for the next three hours. In other war games, this slide is shown for a minute, and we move on. At the end of the exhausting debate, one person approached me during the coffee break and asked me, "Is it like this with other companies?" I answered, "No, not even close." The issue was with the organization's culture, as this kind of debate was encouraged by senior management. They wanted what they called *a diversity of opinions*, but this was extreme and demoralizing to the entire company.

WHEN A WAR GAME BRINGS DOWN MORALE, TEMPORARILY

Often when a company goes into a war game, they have a hypothesis they feel very confident about, but soon realize if they were to proceed with it, the results would be catastrophic to the company. This definitely brings down the morale, but it should, as there is such a thing as overconfidence in your capabilities. At this point, they must approach the situation differently by asking themselves, "What options do we have at our disposal, given our situation? How does it compare to the competition?" This fosters different ways of looking at the marketplace and rebuilds morale around a realistic plan.

ORGANIZE YOUR TEAMS

TEAM RULES

- **NO MORE THAN 6 TEAMS**
  - 3 to 5 teams is optimal
  - Consider including a customer team
- **5-8 PEOPLE PER TEAM**
  - Small teams don't generate heat; large teams can't complete the work in the allotted time
- **TEAM MEMBERS MUST STAY FOR THE ENTIRE GAME**
  - No dropping out—and absolutely no dropping in, even if it's the CEO
- **CROSS FUNCTIONAL TEAMS**
  - 6 marketing people will not be as rigorous as a mixed team
  - Include ex-employees of competitors and people from finance and operations
  - Include people from out in the field

Now it's time to organize your key stakeholders onto teams for your war game, considering morale and skill sets, which we've already discussed. You will make sure your teams are cross-functional, with balanced personalities as well as balanced seniority. This ensures that there's diversity of thought and that everyone contributes.

THE CALCULATION

- **1-6 TEAMS PER GAME**
- **IDEAL SIZE IS 6 PER TEAM**
- **TEAM SIZE CAN RANGE BETWEEN 4 AND 8**

Whether or not you decide to tell everyone which team they are on before the war game comes down to two schools of thought:

1. Tell them

Some clients want to tell players which teams they're on a week in advance to give them enough preparation time to look into the companies they're representing, in order to be prepared for the game.

2. Don't tell them

Other clients say they want players to be on their toes. They don't find out about their teams and companies they're representing until they walk into the room. This is the approach we take with our students.

Every team should be comprised of the following roles:

TEAM LEAD

The team leader should *not* be someone who's in a leadership position in the company, because they tend to dominate the conversations.

NOTETAKER

This person is the team player responsible for writing down the ideas that come up in the breakouts. You should be able to read their handwriting. If you're notetaking electronically, this person needs to be comfortable with people watching them as they type.

TIMEKEEPER

You need one within each team, to stay on track during breakouts. Rounds tend to go fast, and players always think they have more time than they do. But if the timekeeper allots fifteen minutes per question, the game is kept at an even pace.

TEAM PRESENTER

For each round, the teams should appoint a different person to present their strategies to the other teams and judges, to give everyone a chance.

DECIDE WHOM YOUR TEAMS WILL REPRESENT

Consider including your distributors, suppliers and even your customers in your war game as you ideate your teams.

One client we had was a major insurance company with a strong portfolio of personal lines. The company sells largely through independent agents. They wanted to understand the likely consequences of the merger between Travelers Insurance and St. Paul (two of their competitors) with a special focus on any technology-based initiatives the newly merged company could undertake to encourage independent agents to offer it business.

We included a team representing independent agents, along with other teams representing the newly merged competitor, a regional insurance company, and Progressive insurance. Our client gained a clear sense of how the merger would affect the actions of both St. Paul Travelers and the other players. The understanding resulted in a shift in its own strategy for attracting business from independent agents.

When you organize your teams, you'll want to, of course, represent your competition, but you might also include other players who will factor into what type of war game you are having. For example, the strategic war game above was about a long-term play encompassing not just the competition, but the independent agents, or the distributor, whom the client wanted to attract. This gave them an idea of how the independent agents would respond.

You'll also want to pay close attention to niche competition and heretofore quiet competition. In most industries, there are a modest number of large market segments, but there may be numerous niche segments. The niches frequently remain relatively stable, so when they change, it is often a challenge for the players to adapt.

One client provided a highly specialized medical product normally used in intensive care units (ICUs). Apart from the products of one large but relatively passive competitor, there were no substitutes for our client's product. Then a new entrant came into their space with a product that was comparable to our client's. The new competitor was a threat, because it had the ability to bundle its me-too product with a wide range of products used in both the ICU and elsewhere in hospitals. We ran a war game to help the client decide whether and how it should adjust its pricing and its message to hospital-based buyers, of course, including the new competitor, but we wanted to make sure we had a team representing their quiet competitor as well. The client made a sound decision based on the insights gained from teams that represented both the actions of the new entrant and the likely responses of the hitherto quiet competitor with whom our client had shared the market.

FOR YOUR WAR GAME YOU ALSO NEED...

CORE FACILITATOR

This person will be responsible for designing the workshop with the appropriate exercises. As each team already has a lead, this person will lead the groups when they all come together for presentations and for collaboration. The facilitator is masterful at not letting people shut down and can foster a creative environment conducive to brainstorming.

WAR GAME FACILITATION—WHAT'S INVOLVED

- **Adapting to Group Dynamics:** Read the room and adjust the approach based on the energy, engagement levels, and dynamics of the participants.

- **Setting Objectives:** Clearly defining the goals and objectives of the workshop helps participants understand the purpose and stay focused on the desired outcomes.

- **Managing Time:** Responsible for keeping the workshop on schedule, allocating time for different activities, and making adjustments as needed.

- **Encouraging Participation:** Engage all participants by using various techniques to involve introverted or less vocal members and prevent any one person from dominating the conversation.

- **Guiding Discussions:** Lead group discussions, ensuring that all participants have the opportunity to express their thoughts, ideas, and concerns.

- **Creating a Safe Environment:** Establish a respectful and inclusive atmosphere, encouraging open communication and making participants feel comfortable sharing their opinions.

- **Summarizing and Synthesizing:** Recap key points and insights from discussions, helping participants consolidate their understanding and move forward effectively.

- **Asking Powerful Questions:** Thought-provoking questions stimulate deeper thinking, foster creativity, and encourage participants to consider different perspectives.

- **Maintaining Focus:** Steer conversations back on track if discussions veer off-topic, ensuring that the workshop remains aligned with its objectives.

- **Encouraging Action Steps:** Guide participants in identifying actionable steps and commitments that can be taken following the workshop.

- **Flexibility:** Adapt the workshop plan if unexpected issues arise or if participants express specific needs.

- **Managing Group Energy:** Monitoring the energy level of the group and incorporating energizing activities or breaks helps maintain engagement and enthusiasm.

- **Cultivating a Learning Environment:** Foster an environment of continuous learning, where participants feel encouraged to explore new ideas and challenge their existing knowledge.

- **Conflict Resolution:** Address conflicts or disagreements that may arise during discussions and guide the group toward constructive resolutions.

Please note that biased facilitators can destroy the process. For this reason, it's important that the facilitator doesn't have a vested interest in the war game topics. For example, in a war game we ran for a large supply chain company, the senior vice president was nominated to be the facilitator, but he already had strong opinions on what the company should do. In the brainstorming round, he was influencing the discussions, but more disastrously, in the main room discussions he was commenting on team outputs and not letting the teams objectively share their analysis or have productive discussions. This became very apparent to the participants, and they shut down for most of the war game.

Consider bringing in a neutral third party who can bring up subjects during the workshop that may be delicate issues or even taboo, but which also must be brought out on the table in order to achieve your goals. We have pioneering experience in organizing and facilitating war games, strategy workshops, and scenario analyses, ensuring that the exercise runs smoothly and without distractions. We'll integrate our previous experience with preparing and running other workshops into your game.

JUDGES

The leadership team in your organization is best for these roles, or you can invite external experts from your industry to evaluate each round. Having a panel of judges helps provide teams with objective feedback on their strategies instantly. You can even turn the war game into a competition with a prize at the end for the winning team.

TIMEKEEPER

You have timekeepers on teams for the breakouts, but you also need a timekeeper that keeps the entire war game on track. This can also be the facilitator.

NOTETAKER FOR WAR GAME

This person is important and should not be on any team, as they will need to take detailed notes during the brainstorming round of your war game, when all the players ideate strategies for your Playbook.

In a physical environment, your notetaker can go low tech (flip charts, markers, Post-it Notes, printed out templates) or can go high tech (iPads, electronic white boards, Google docs, PowerPoints).

I prefer to take technology out of the equation and use old-fashioned brainstorming. The drawback to technology is you are inhibited by the notetaker's ability to type. You can also be limited by the technology if it backfires.

Now that your Briefing Book is done, you've taken stock of your resources, and thoughtfully organized your teams, it's time to start creating your Scenario Book by ideating scenarios and tactics for each round of your war game.

Refer to page 208 in the appendix for this chapter's template or scan the QR code in the appendix to download a full set of the printable digital templates for this book.

CHAPTER 12

DECIDING ON SCENARIOS AND TACTICS

I n 2006, Massachusetts passed health care reform legislation to provide coverage to all residents. They wanted to reduce costs to the state, which had been paying hospitals for the emergency medical costs of the uninsured. The legislation required all adults to obtain coverage from private carriers if they didn't get coverage from their employers, and it imposed state income tax penalties on anyone who was uninsured. Carriers were encouraged to offer affordable premiums for older uninsured residents and raise them slightly for younger people. Employers who didn't offer insurance that met minimum standards had to subsidize employees who purchased individual plans. The state subsidized premiums for low-income people.

No one could predict whether the plan would work, or what the consequences would be to providers, employers, and payers. We ran a scenario analysis for a carrier that was worried about how to respond in the face of this uncertainty. The scenario analysis resulted in four drivers that would determine the short and long-term success of the reform. Then we led the company's leadership team through a "strategic implications" war game in which they identified specific strategies they needed to implement in any event. For example, the client substantially increased its marketing and altered its message to appeal to the younger uninsured individuals who would be drawn into the market. The leadership team also identified contingent strategies that could be implemented as the picture became clearer. As a capstone, a core team continued to monitor the four drivers for indicators that would trigger the contingent strategies.

This is what happens when a company creates scenarios and strategies for how to respond to big *what-ifs* in the market.

Here's what happens when companies aren't prepared:

I recently read about a pharmaceutical product that had been brought to market in the ophthalmology space. Shortly after, I saw a direct-to-consumer advertisement promoting the product. Then I read an article on Endpoints News which said that the company's stock price dropped 21 percent, because a few physicians cited safety issues with the new drug.

This event is a very tangible scenario in a tactical war game for a pharmaceutical company launching a new product in the market. The question: What would be the effect of a safety signal and are we prepared to deal with it?

The statements that the company made after their stock dropped were to the effect of, "We're looking into this. We're working through this," which didn't signify that they were prepared at all.

When you have a strategy, whether it's tactical execution, operational, or strategic, ask yourself what is the most disruptive event that could happen? And consequently, are you prepared for it? This disruptive event is called a *scenario*. Scenarios are ways to stress test your strategies in a war game environment.

If you pitch your worst-case scenario to your leadership team and they respond, "Oh, that's never going to happen," that's reason enough to war game it. Because the bottom line with scenarios is that nobody really knows if they will happen. The more farfetched a particular event might be, the more people tend to think it won't happen, and sometimes they're wrong.

"Scenarios are intended to help companies think about their market through a range of possible future options. They form a shared basis for strategic conversations by exploring uncertainties to make successful decisions."
—CHAIRMAN, LARGE RETAIL COMPANY

BEST-CASE SCENARIOS VERSUS WORST-CASE SCENARIOS

People generally tend to think about worst-case events, but you can also look at best-case events and get ready to respond. Scenarios explore a range of different future negative and positive options in terms of which way the industry, the marketplace, and the competitive environment could go.

Best-case scenarios, of course, get a lot less attention, because nobody questions good news, and worst-case scenarios put everyone into defensive mode. But the point of war-gaming scenarios is to get out of offensive or defensive mode for a moment, so that you can honestly reflect on what to do either way.

So why war game a best-case scenario? Because even best-case scenarios could be disastrous, if you aren't ready. What if you introduce a product into the marketplace and your sales are significantly higher than you anticipated? A great example is the diabetes drug, *Ozempic*, which is also being used for weight loss. But Novo Nordisk couldn't meet this market demand with their supply, and now consumers who need the product for its original intention can't get it.

The questions I would put before them in a war game are: Do you anticipate increased demand for your product? Is your manufacturing capable of producing more product? Are you able to distribute it? Do you have plans in place so you can capitalize on this event? And then, do you have longer-term strategies to ensure your strategy is sustainable versus the short-term response?

When most corporations ideate scenarios, everyone automatically thinks about the world ending. But sometimes scenarios could mean that the world is giving you a huge opportunity. The question for you is as follows: Are you and your company ready to capitalize on that?

SCENARIOS AND THE THREE TYPES OF WAR GAMES

A common mistake that a lot of organizations make is only creating scenarios for longer-term strategies. You can also use them for short-term planning. In fact, scenario planning fits into all three types of war games, but the types of scenarios that you would use differ for each:

- *Tactical* short-term scenarios help you figure out how to win, more specifically what will impede your ability to execute as you go to market.

- *Operational* short- to mid-term scenarios tend to be around more issues like your competition and your competitive environment.

- *Strategic* long-term scenarios are a future look at macroeconomic factors that will affect your competitive environment farther down the line.

SCENARIO-PLANNING PROCESSES

The process that you would use for going through scenario planning can be as complicated or as simple as you make it, depending on how much time you have for your war game.

In my courses, I ask students to quickly go through a twenty-minute scenario-planning exercise for a case example. Most of the content that they produce makes sense. Conversely, I've held corporate war games where the scenario-planning process took six months, as it was much more detailed and deliberate in terms of research.

For your war-gaming environment, your process comes down to how much time you've allotted for your game. If time is short, you can pre-populate your war game by having a separate team research market disruptions and come up with a list of scenarios that the teams will then respond to, or if you have more time, you can do it in the game itself.

Each approach has benefits. If you have your teams brainstorm scenarios in the war game, they have ownership over the insights that they've generated themselves. But in certain instances, you can give teams deeply researched scenarios to open their minds to new information they may not be privy to.

QUICK THREE-STEP PROCESS FOR IN-GAME SCENARIO PLANNING

For the purposes of war gaming, you go through this twenty-minute, three-step process and quickly build scenarios.

Step 1: After a few rounds of strategy ask your teams:

- Based on the external insights that you've generated so far, what would be the most disruptive event in this marketplace?

- What would be disruptive to our company?

- What would be disruptive to the other teams?

- What would be disruptive to key stakeholders in that environment?

Step 2: Give everyone a Post-it Note and a few minutes to fill it out, and then ask them to stick their notes onto a wall. With twenty to forty people in the room, you very quickly see themes emerge in terms of what those potential disruptive scenarios might be.

Step 3: Then you ask the participants to vote, choosing the top two to four disruptive things they see on the wall.

Now you have scenarios you can war game in your next round.

IDEATING SCENARIOS ON THE FLY

Let's say, for example, you're a technology company doing a tactical war game, and halfway through you start to realize that your customers are really interested in your underlying tech and not so much your product. This happens all the time—but it's no occasion to panic.

General insights always come from a war-gaming exercise, which, of course, is why we do them.

At that point, based on your strategic objectives and the way that the market is likely to evolve, you might ideate new strategies on the fly. Given that this is risky, you will want to take a few minutes and come up with some new scenarios and war game those. Or, you may have the need to revisit new scenarios six months or one year later, on a periodic level. Again, this is very common. Many of the most sophisticated companies do scenario planning and war gaming regularly, rather than as a one-off exercise, because they always see a need to keep updating their strategies based on ever-changing markets.

We had a client who wanted to conduct war games to roll out a new product in all 200 countries it operated in. They had done a proof-of-concept in a few countries and then wanted to use war games to construct their strategic Playbooks across the globe. One of the first war games was in Korea, where there was an impending regulation change that could increase the price of products in their category. The initial reaction to the regulation was negative throughout the company. They war gamed scenarios where they tried to work around the price increase. But, during the war game there was a realization that this was, in fact, an opportunity to differentiate premium products from other non-premium products. In fact, by running scenarios for the competition's likely strategies during the war game, they came to understand that the competition viewed this change positively. As a result, the company identified a huge opportunity to increase prices for their premium products in conjunction with the new regulations. They war gamed the new scenario, and after it proved to be successful, put it in their Playbook, took action on it and met with success.

FIVE-STEP PROCESS FOR IN-DEPTH SCENARIO PLANNING

If you really want to get deep into this process, many books have been written about scenario planning.[33] The intent is to think through what level of scenarios you need to bring into these games to make sure that you're prepared for unknown situations, i.e., that you have contingency plans in place. You either look at events that might happen, or other risks and opportunities presenting themselves in your competitive marketplace.

To illustrate the process, I'm going to use a Scenario Book my company created (based on the Shell methodology) for a large clothing and home goods manufacturer in Hong Kong. The key question was the following: We supply some of the biggest retailers in the world: What if we're serving the dinosaurs? What if retail changes in the future and the chain stores that we supply are less relevant?

We put a team together from key stakeholders in their organization, and before their game, pinpointed the six biggest drivers for retail, sectioning them into two super-drivers, and four others. Since we had more time, we also listed the constituent elements for each driver, i.e., current status and causality. We plotted the extremes for each on a pole and plotted where we were and where the market was going, using red and green dots. In essence, we created a world for each driver that naturally led to scenarios.

Finally, we war gamed out the top scenarios to help build strategies for the future of the business that were there.

Here was our five-step process for creating scenarios, before the war game:

---

33   "Shell scenarios," Shell Global, accessed August 2023, https://www.shell.com/energy-and-innovation/the-energy-future/scenarios.html.

STEP ONE: LIST ALL YOUR *KEY DRIVERS*

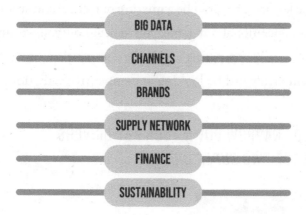

- Key drivers come from impact to your marketplace. What impactful events may occur? What are the key uncertainties? What can you glean from external trends happening right now?

- These could be regulatory, economic, technology, internal, or external, such as pricing pressure, depending on your war game (see below).

Key drivers broken down by war game type:

STRATEGIC

For this type of war game, you would look at dynamic macroeconomic factors. These could be regulatory, economic, technology, and social changes.

TACTICAL

These key drivers are around shorter-term, go-to-market events. The more tactical you get, the more you see elements of a marketing mix, such as product price and promotion.

OPERATIONAL

These key factors could be a mixture of tactical and strategic. For an operational war game, you look at how your company is holistically competing versus the competition, or within a certain area you'd be looking at competitive activities.

STEP TWO: NARROW DOWN YOUR KEY DRIVERS TO YOUR TOP TWO *SUPER DRIVERS*

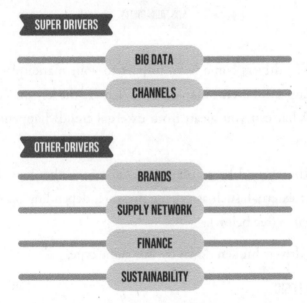

SUPER DRIVERS

BIG DATA

CHANNELS

OTHER-DRIVERS

BRANDS

SUPPLY NETWORK

FINANCE

SUSTAINABILITY

You won't have time to war game all your key drivers (more on that below). The quickest way to narrow this down is have your team vote on these key drivers in relation to biggest possible impact to your business, then rank them in order of votes.

Then section them into your top two *Super Drivers,* i.e., the top ranked events you know will have the most impact on your industry, and then put the rest into *Other Key Drivers,* i.e., events that still have an impact, yet not as much.

STEP THREE: CREATE *A* TO *B* END STATE POLES FOR YOUR SUPER DRIVERS

When you create poles for each key factor, you think in end states, or best and worse-case outcomes, plotting one extreme at A and the other at B. Start with your two Super Drivers. For example, the *Brands* key driver in the above graphic questions how retail shoppers will consider individual brands in the future. On *Pole A*, we see that brands are prized by the customer, but on the opposite end, *Pole B*, we see that brands aren't valued at all.

Keep in mind that if each key driver creates two scenarios, in the interest of time you might not be able to war game all of them. If you create poles for your two Super Drivers, you will have four possible scenarios for your war game.

STEP FOUR: CREATE AN X- AND Y-AXIS GRAPH WITH YOUR POLES

Now, simple enough, you cross your two poles, creating a grid of four squares or scenarios.

LIST OF DRIVERS

- Sourcing
- Technological Advancements
- New Players

- Customer Expectations
- Sustainability & Environmental Concerns
- E-commerce Growth

- Last-mile Delivery Challenges
- Pricing
- Monthly Membership

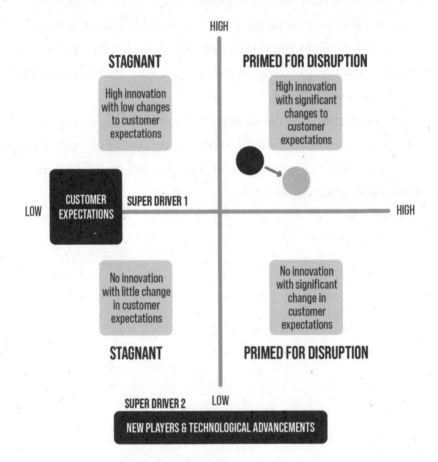

As you can see from the above example, our two Super Drivers, Customer Expectations and New Players for Technological Advances, made four quadrants, each with a positive outcome and a negative outcome. For example, if Customer Expectations are low, but Innovation is high (top left quadrant), this would be an instance of wasted potential in your market. However, if Customer Expectations are high and Innovation is low (bottom right quadrant), the market is primed for disruption.

At this point, you could war game all four of these scenarios, or you could narrow it down further by moving to the next step.

STEP FIVE (OPTIONAL): PLOT YOUR GREEN AND RED DOTS ON YOUR GRAPH

For this step, if you choose to narrow down your scenarios, you look at each quadrant and ask yourself: *Where is the world right now?* Depending on where you think the market is, you place a green dot.

Now you ask yourself, *Where is the world heading?* Based on which direction you think the world is going, you place a red dot.

As you can see in the graph, the teams here felt that the market was poised for revolution, with Customer Expectations and Innovation both being currently at an all-time high and headed for more of the same. This is one scenario we later war gamed.

In some cases, you may not have your green and red dots in the same quadrant, so this would give you two scenarios you have to plan for. One is where the world is today and the second is where the world is heading toward. In this situation ask yourself, "Are we prepared for both?" and if the answer is no, then you have some work to do.

Finally, you pull your resulting scenario(s) into your war game and depending on time, repeat with your remaining key drivers.

GETTING STUCK IN THE SCENARIO-PLANNING PROCESS

At this point, all this information on how to plan scenarios has either gotten you excited about creating your Scenario Book, or you're feeling a little overwhelmed. If it's the latter, don't think you're alone in that. You might need to call in some experts to give you an outside point-of-view.

Here's an example:

When we think of disruption, we usually think about the impact of some change in technology, or perhaps a merger of two competitors. In this instance, a distribution market that had been relatively stable for decades was about to be disrupted by the entry of a powerful player from outside the industry. Would there be a wave of consolidation as the incumbent players sought to build scale? Would the new entrant's aggressive timetable cause it to stumble and ultimately withdraw? How would customers respond to the entry of a powerful low-cost outside player with a less-than-spotless reputation?

With all the uncertainty, the top management for a tech company was unable to come to grips with what it needed to do. A scenario analysis was the best way to grapple with the many possible outcomes they could reasonably posit, but they had no idea where to start, so they brought us in to lead a war game for them.

Working with both outside experts and with the client, we agreed on the key drivers that would shape the future and developed a set of rational alternative scenarios for the market using a more in-depth process than the one above. Then we facilitated a strategy workshop for the client's senior leadership team. A set of clear tasks emerged through the rounds and the players all brainstormed a set of contingent strategies to deal with the unknowns. The scenario analysis helped the management team get past their lack of consensus and deal with the imminent changes in its market.

DECIDING HOW MANY SCENARIOS PER WAR GAME

In general, the fewer scenarios you have, the more manageable your game will be. In the last exercise, we took the top two Super Drivers and built four scenarios from those. Certain companies do much more involved scenario planning, so instead of two Super Drivers and four scenarios, they might plot the four key drivers, ending up with sixteen scenarios. That's way too much for most organizations to deal with in a one- to two-day war game.

Each round in a war game usually lasts about an hour. Most companies can war game two to three scenarios in a round, at twenty to thirty minutes each.

I'll break it down. If, for example, you're doing a day-and-a-half workshop, the format would look like this:

- Introduction

- Each team builds and roleplays base case strategies

- Each team decides upon their go-to-market strategy

- 1–2 rounds of scenarios to stress test the strategies (4–6 scenarios)

- The teams come together and align on key competitive themes and finalize their Playbook

We conducted a war game for the manufacturer of one of the largest diabetes products in the world, whom we were very familiar with as we had been working in their market for several years. We told them, "Your team fully understands your strategy and given what we all know, going through base case strategies is not going to be the most optimal use of your time. However, a lot of unknowns exist in your space." As a result, the whole workshop was responding to eight scenarios in one day. Each of the teams would compare and contrast the responses. Even though this wasn't typical, what we already knew helped us determine how many scenarios were useful in the war game.

As you become more familiar with war gaming and integrate it into your regular planning process, you won't see the need to formalize the process each time. Some companies, like Shell, will encounter a threat or opportunity, create a few scenarios, and then war game them for half a day.

Shell has incorporated scenarios into their planning process since the 1970s. In fact, when the oil shocks happened in the 1970s, Shell had already gamed scenarios very similar to that, and as a result they were prepared for that situation.

Years ago, we conducted a tactical war game for a pharmaceutical company launching a new product. One of the scenarios in the workshop was: What if the FDA doesn't approve your drug?

You can imagine the shock in the room. Nobody wanted to talk about that happening.

But that's the whole point of scenarios—talking about things that nobody wants to talk about. As I mentioned before, people love the good news scenarios. The bad news scenarios are where you get pushback. We heard protests like: "Our data packet is superior!" and "We had clinical studies with thousands of patients!"

In spite of this, they did war game that scenario and built a plan. Four or five months later, the FDA did not approve their product. Instead of panicking, they went to the plan in their Playbook. They immediately took action, resubmitted the application, and then the product got approved.

That product later became their best-selling drug with over $1 billion in sales.

When I worked for another pharmaceutical company, we held a strategic war game regarding the future of healthcare in the US. We went through building scenarios in a very involved, months-long process. Then we war gamed the scenarios and created a very robust Playbook, which they never used.

The company filed for bankruptcy in early 2023.

If your company is going into a war game and the scenario is scary, you can take the attitude that there's no way we can survive this, or you can war game a solution by using the resources that you have. This is a time for thinking creatively, brainstorming, and innovating. In the end, your team will know exactly what the plan is to compete, and win. This is why the next two chapters are so crucial. In chapter 13, we will talk about holding your war game so that you get the best possible outcomes for your Playbook.

Refer to 209 in the appendix for this chapter's template or scan the QR code in the appendix to download a full set of the printable digital templates for this book.

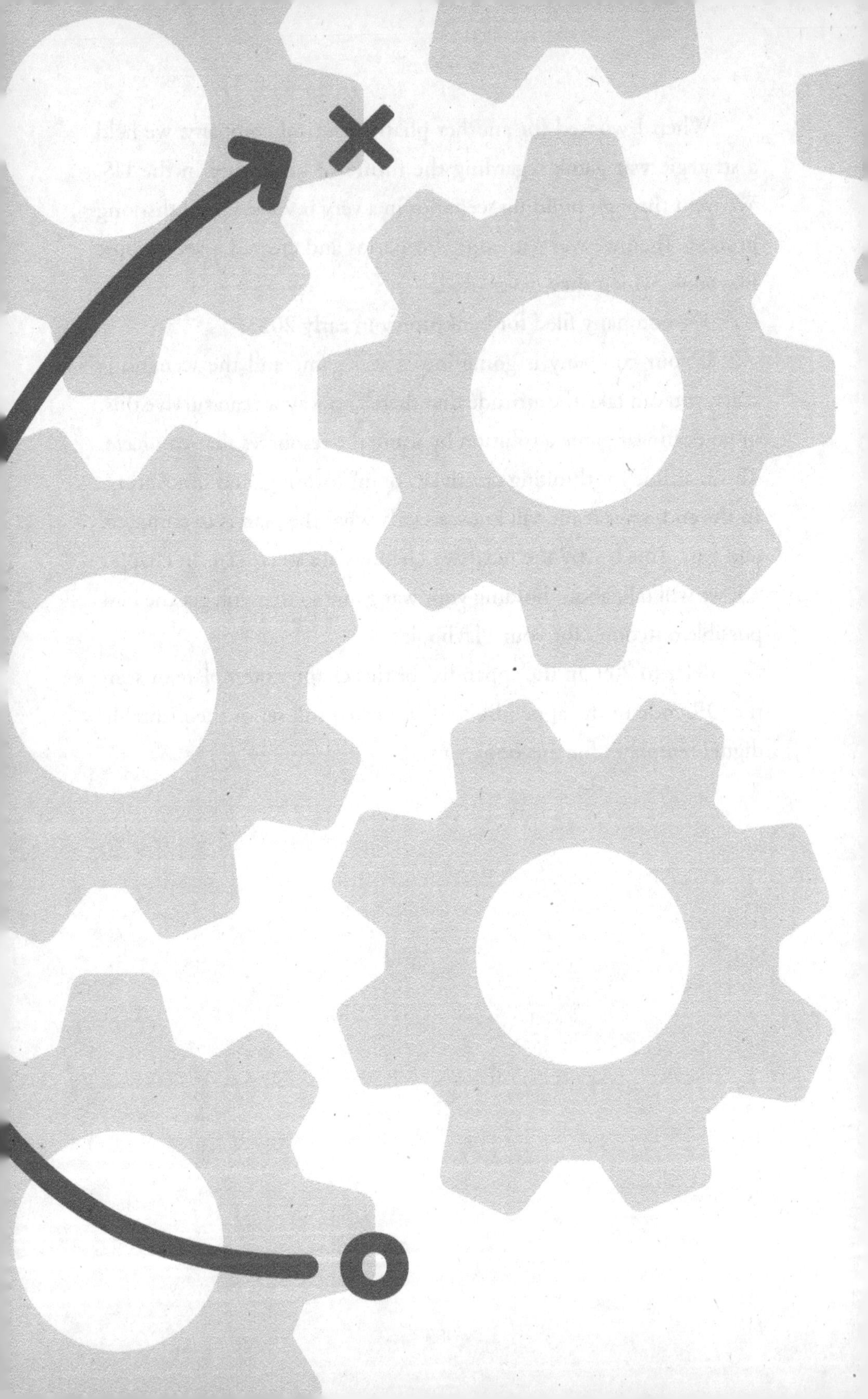

CONDUCTING THE WAR GAME

W e have a client who manufactures infant formula and sells it across the globe, both in industrialized countries and in emerging markets. Infant formula marketing, labeling, and promotion is driven in most countries by the World Health Organization (WHO) guidelines. As regulations have tightened, each company in the market has responded by segmenting products for toddlers and young children and by introducing variants of traditional powdered formula, or by adding other forms of product line extensions to differentiate themselves.

Our client wanted to understand the likely future actions of its major global and regional competitors as the regulation got even more restrictive. We ran a war game for them with regulatory scenarios that resulted in two competitive teams merging and a third competitor promoting in emerging markets while flouting regulatory restrictions.

In the final round, all the players brainstormed for their Playbook detailing two main strategies: the company would introduce new products that leapfrogged their competitors, and would improve upon a product they already had, all while following the new guidelines. After the war game, our client implemented their Playbook and subsequently succeeded.

Running a war game is no easy task, but if done right, you can create a Playbook for a winning competitive strategy. This chapter will give you all the details and the processes you need to run your war game.

We outline a couple of general structures for different types of war games in this chapter that can be further refined depending on your ultimate objectives and outcomes. But please note, these are general and will change according to your unique needs.

LOGISTICS BEFORE YOUR WAR GAME

Preparing for your war game is just as crucial as the game itself. You want to ensure everything goes smoothly, the teams have fun, and that the outputs generate big competitive wins for your company. This list is by no means exhaustive.

THE ROOMS AND DECOR

Make sure you have the room confirmed. I recently ran a war game for a client who thought they had the room; and then they didn't. The night before, we were scrambling to move the war game from physical to virtual. Fortunately, at the last minute, we got the room, and the workshop was a success.

The room should ideally not be onsite where your offices are, because this can be really distracting, as people pop in and out to check email, or jump into another meeting, or take calls while the game is in play.

You also need to secure breakout rooms for the rounds so teams can strategize privately during each round. You'll need one breakout room per team.

In your main war room, you'll need tables for each team. Ideally, each team will be color coded, for example, a yellow team, a red team, and a green team, each one representing a different company. I had one client who got their ad agency involved, and they branded their war game *The Think Tank*, as in a military tank. They developed templates for the war game with camouflage backgrounds. Everyone wore T-shirts with their team colors and the companies that they were representing printed on them. The meeting room was covered in camouflage decor and all the players received dog tags engraved with their names, their team names, and the event title. I still have the dog tags in my glove compartment fifteen years later!

This made the event more fun, but if you don't have the time or resources, you can simplify with printed name tags, bandannas in the team colors, or paper tablecloths in team colors. I've also seen competitive imagery at each table, such as brochures, recent ad campaigns, and logos.

On each table, have a couple of copies of the Briefing Book available for participants; in case some participants haven't been able to print it out or worse review it before the war game (yikes!).

THE FOOD

Make sure you feed people, or you could get tired and hungry players who aren't good for much. Lots of snacks on the tables also helps keep the energy flowing. A war game client recently said, "I'll be honest with you. At the end of this, people will remember the breakfast and the lunch as a gauge of success."

INFRASTRUCTURE

Depending on whether you want to run your war game low tech or high tech, this is some of the equipment you might need:

- Flip charts

- Post-its

- Pens

- Notebooks

- Templates (you can copy and use the templates in the appendix of this book, or print them with the QR code)

- Projectors people can hook up to laptops

- Wi-Fi depending on how connected you really want people to be

VIRTUAL WAR GAME LOGISTICS

RULES FOR VIRTUAL WAR GAME PLAYERS:

1. NOBODY SHOULD HAVE THEIR CAMERA OFF.

2. WORK IN A PRIVATE, QUIET SPACE ON A PASSWORD PROTECTED WI-FI NETWORK. NO COFFEE SHOPS.

3. NO ATTENDING THE WAR GAME ON YOUR PHONE, AS YOU CAN'T ACCESS INTERACTIVE FUNCTIONS.

Before the pandemic, war games were always conducted in person. But, since then, technology has made it possible to hold virtual war games. When you do this, you must break the war game into smaller chunks, for example, three-hour sessions, so that your players don't get screen fatigue. Take lots of breaks and send either curated snacks or food delivery gift cards so that players can order food for the war game.

TECHNOLOGY

- For a virtual war game, you have multiple options for technology, I prefer Zoom and Microsoft Teams.

- Use breakout rooms in the software for team rounds.

- Use interactive polling software.

- Use interactive whiteboards (they enable people to collaborate in a non-verbal manner).

- Customize backgrounds for each team, with colors and logos.

- Have strong Wi-Fi.

- Have your facilitator use two computers (desktop and laptop) in case one crashes.

- Use password protection for your meeting room (send in war game calendar invite).

- Use a waiting room for your meeting, but then after the start time, drop the meeting room and default to password protection.

PREPARATION BEFORE THE GAME

A week before the war game:

- send out the Briefing Book and the team assignments;

- send customized background they will need to upload to their meeting software;

- remind your players of your objectives, expectations, and key questions; and

- go through parts of the Briefing Book, making sure people are comfortable with it.

WAR GAME DURATION

A typical in-person war game is conducted over one or two days. The most common duration for an in-person war game is a day and a half and is preferable, as it gives enough time to have in-depth discussions and is less hurried. One-day war games are more compressed and are considered in situations where a company may not be able to bring a large group of participants together for a longer duration. The duration you choose will also determine how many rounds of war gaming you can include in the game.

Virtual war games are now also very popular as well as they save on travel costs and time. Virtual war games are structured differently; instead of a day or two, they are generally broken into three-hour sessions over a few days to avoid screen fatigue for the participants.

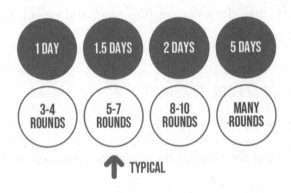

WAR GAME STRUCTURE

Now we will talk about the structure of your war game. This would be the same whether you are physical or virtual, with the difference being the total time allocated to the game will determine the number of rounds of war gaming you can conduct.

Outlined below are war games with four rounds that you can easily conduct in a day; if you have more time, you can add additional rounds to gain even deeper insights into the topics you are war gaming.

THE INTRODUCTION

One of the largest diabetes drug manufacturers in the world was getting into a new market they were unfamiliar with. They needed to process a significant amount of information to have a productive war game. They spent four hours on the introduction for the war game, going over their objectives, giving context for the market, outlining what was happening from a developmental perspective.

This was an exception, as usually the introduction is about fifteen minutes to an hour. Your introduction is an opportunity to do a company-wide mini training. It's the ultimate teaching tool in the sense that you're giving knowledge, and then applying it immediately after in a war game setting to really solidify it.

To kick off your war game, have the most senior person in the company do an introduction. They will set the right tone for the meeting in terms of the importance and expectation.

They might:

1. thank everyone for their time,

2. reiterate the winning objective,

3. state the reasons why this is an important initiative for the company,

4. state what the desired outputs are,

5. describe how they will be implemented, and

6. review some key points from the Briefing Book.

After the introduction, the facilitator can tell everyone, "You've been 'fired' and are going to work for the competition. You get a thank you note and a twenty-five-cent key chain with the company logo as a thank you for your service. Take your knowledge of this company to your new job working for the competition and think through your base case strategies."

Now your teams will break into their individual rooms to get to work. I will show you a general structure for a strategic war game, where you want to broadly understand your competitive environment and use some scenarios to stress test various situations. The last round is critical to include to ensure you get to actionable insights. But this is just a general outline. Your structure might differ according to time and your objectives.

BASE CASE STRATEGIES: ROUNDS ONE AND TWO

The first round is the warm-up for participants, for the teams to get into the minds of the competition. You might not get many insights at this point, but it will help participants to start thinking like the companies they represent. In round one, the teams will discuss their representative companies, what their winning aspirations are, capabilities, assumptions and then develop their base case strategies.

After each round, each team will present their outputs when they return to the main war room, allowing all the teams to compare and contrast the different approaches in the marketplace.

Round two is around how they will execute on their winning strategy and what actions they will take to do so in the marketplace.

It's important at this stage that when they're talking about the company that they're representing they don't say "This company will do this," but rather, "We will do this." It's a very subtle difference, but it makes a huge difference in the quality of the outputs. Owning the company causes players to look through an inside-out competitive lens versus an outside in.

The Briefing Books already have information on the companies, the capabilities for each, and the assumptions each company makes about the marketplace. The teams will review the information about their companies and think about the future for the company that they represent. They can answer the following questions:

1. What is your winning aspiration and how are you planning on getting there?

2. What is your company likely to do in the future in the short term and for the long term?

3. How are you going to attack the other teams?

After the second round in the main room, you can have a discussion around key insights the teams generated, thinking about where some of the biggest impacts are.

Next, you will war game the scenarios. The facilitator will propose the first and let the teams adjourn to their private rooms.

SCENARIOS: ROUND THREE

In this round, teams will identify potential problems that they might have by taking into account their winning aspirations, gaps in their capabilities, morale and resources, which they will reference in their toolkit from the Briefing Book. After carefully weighing in these factors, each team will decide how to respond to each scenario.

University students play two- to three-round war games, leaving one round for scenarios, with each scenario taking about twenty to thirty minutes (that means two to three scenarios in this round).

In a corporate environment, you would do a minimum of four rounds in the war game, leaving room for two rounds of scenarios (four to six scenarios total, as I mentioned in chapter 12). Some corporations war game up to ten rounds depending on how much time they have and what their objectives are. For the purposes of this section, we will limit it to one round.

After each team hears the scenario, they will decide, in creating their go-to-market strategy, if they want to declare war, retreat, counterattack, or surrender.

- *Declaring war:* Is yours a marketplace that your company is likely to disrupt? Can you change the market terms and shake things up?

- *Retreat:* For some companies, it makes sense from a strategic perspective to pick and choose your battles. In this sense you back off, giving your competition something in exchange for a bigger attack later.

- *Counterattack:* X (formally Twitter) and Meta/Threads is a great example of a counterattack, where Threads is Meta's attempt to make a better product than what X is offering disgruntled users.

- *Surrender:* In certain instances, you see that a particular scenario would make it impossible for your company to make money in your market, so you would opt to save your resources and get out.

INTERNAL ALIGNMENT AND ACTIONS: FINAL ROUND

At the start of the final round, your teams will all come together and collectively brainstorm on behalf of your company. No more representing the competition. The facilitator will tell players, "Leaving the company was a bad dream. You're still working for your company. As compensation for the trauma that you've been through, HR will double your salary." Everyone's now aligned in terms of the biggest threats, opportunities, and actions.

What each team will now consider, now from *your* company's perspective, are these types of questions:

- What are the core implications of the rounds of war gaming we have just been through?

- What did we learn from going through the various scenarios?

- What are the core actions we need to take?

- What are the things we need to consider doing in response to the scenarios?

- How will we beat the competition in the marketplace?

This is where notetaking becomes crucial. As I mentioned in chapter 11, I like to use a low-tech approach for this round, as it moves quickly. The notetaker can write the answers on separate walls, segmented by opportunities and risks, so you can see themes arise, as well as get a map of the marketplace.

Here is an example of a more tactical war game structure. You'll notice some differences in the exercises as the objectives here are more around execution and how to win.

EXAMPLE OUTLINE OF A FOUR-ROUND TACTICAL WAR GAME (FOR PRODUCT DIFFERENTIATION / GO TO MARKET)

1. **PRODUCT DIFFERENTIATION**

   a. The benefits ladder: What are the physical attributes of your product? What are the functional attributes? What are the emotional benefits of your product?

   b. Messaging statements for key stakeholders: Create positioning statements for this segment of the marketplace, e.g., our product offers this, and here're the reasons to believe.

2. **DEVELOP GO-TO-MARKET STRATEGY (SALES, MARKETING, DISTRIBUTION, ETC.)**

3. **RESPOND TO POTENTIAL DISRUPTIVE SCENARIOS (FROM YOUR TEAM'S PERSPECTIVE), AND THEN TURN IT BACK INTO OPPORTUNITIES AND RISKS.**

4. **ACTIONS: EVERYONE NOW LOOKS AT IT FROM THE HOME TEAM'S PERSPECTIVE**

   a. What actions will you take? What do you do now? Pick and choose which ones are appropriate for your objectives.

   b. Finalize Competitive Playbook

ENSURING WAR GAME SUCCESS

These are some challenges I've encountered in my years of running war games. If you know what to look for, you can prevent it. This list is by no means exhaustive.

LEADERSHIP DOESN'T BUY INTO THE WAR GAME

As I mentioned earlier, you want your most senior leader to do the introduction in order to set the right tone. If that doesn't happen, it can really throw things off by disrupting morale. We had one instance where the senior person gave the introduction, saying that the war game was irrelevant for what they were doing, but it would be interesting to see what everyone came up with. Sadly, the participants treated the workshop as interesting, and the war game did not change anything. The outputs were not actionable. War games, as I mentioned before, are not interesting workshops. They are actionable workshops.

FACILITATOR TOO INVESTED

The facilitator can be overly invested in what the teams are doing. It is the teams' responsibility to come up with content, so they have alignment and ownership. I've seen instances of overly animated facilitators in war games where I was involved but wasn't facilitating. They were biased toward the content, taking a preference for one team versus another. It impeded innovation and created an inaccurate picture of what the competition would have been devising.

POOR TIME MANAGEMENT

You must make sure that you allocate enough time for your war game so that you can get to the actionable final round, where you collectively ideate the strategies for your Playbook. This last round is the difference between an interesting and an actionable workshop.

It's great to do the analysis of the competition, but it's most important to get to the implications and the strategy that arises from that. I had a client who, at the end of one of the workshops, said to me, "This has been the most effective war game I've ever seen, because it drove action at the end."

The final round is where you get alignment and prioritization on what the next steps will be. Stopping halfway is a huge pitfall. I had another client that initially wanted a day-and-a-half workshop, and later said, "We don't have a day and a half. Can we do it in one day?" I agreed. Then the client said, "We can't do it in one day. Can we do it in six hours?" When I arrived to conduct the war game, the client said, "We don't have six hours. We're running behind our agenda. Can we do this in two hours?" It was the worst war game ever.

TOO LONG OF A BRIEFING BOOK

Briefing Books, back when I started war gaming, used to be 100- to 150-page Word documents. The burden to create the document was significant. But the burden to consume the document was even worse. The result was a very small percentage of people read it and came prepared for the workshop.

Later, we transitioned the Briefing Book to a more visual, graphics-heavy PowerPoint presentation. For your war game, you don't have to spend too much time making it look aesthetically pleasing. The main thing is to keep the Briefing Book as brief and succinct as possible, according to your audience.

If your players are very familiar with the market and competition, your Briefing Book will be much more to the point than that for a team new to the market. As I mentioned above, you can make use of the introduction, with slides and multimedia, to acclimate teams to a new space.

MISSING ELEMENTS TO THE BRIEFING BOOK OR NONE AT ALL

Doing a workshop without a Briefing Book is like driving a car with your eyes closed. You need to have a common understanding among your players. I once observed a war game on strategy planning for a business unit of a large financial services company. They didn't have a Briefing Book and consequently spent more time looking for information than engaging in discussions and brainstorming, which made the war game a failure.

I held a war game for an incumbent player in the financial market being challenged by next-generation fintech companies. They were bringing in new technologies at the time, like cloud computing. For the incumbent, a glossary was important in their Briefing Book to introduce new terms they never used internally, because their systems and processes were radically different.

LACK OF ALIGNMENT ON TEAMS

The best-case scenario is that everyone on the team agrees. But often, half the team decides the attack is going to be this, and the other half declares that they don't have the resources for that. Then there's a big argument about whether the team's capabilities and resources line up with one strategy or another.

At this point, the facilitator needs to get the team to vote.

Fortunately, lack of alignment is very unusual. If you've created a robust Briefing Book it helps achieve alignment, in that all the facts and data are right there.

Now that you've created some scenarios, and held your war game, let's discuss the single-most important output to your war game—the Playbook. Taking action on your Playbook is what makes an interesting war game actionable.

Refer to pages 210-212 in the appendix for this chapter's templates or scan the QR code in the appendix to download a full set of the printable digital templates for this book and bonus content containing examples of different war game structures.

CHAPTER 14

MOVING FROM WAR ROOM TO REAL WORLD

When we think of disruption, we usually think about the impact of a new technology or a merger between two big competitors. A major distributor from a stable market was about to be disrupted, for the first time in decades, by the entry of a powerful player from outside the industry. With all this uncertainty, top management couldn't come to grips with what to do, so they brought us in to war game. Gaming a scenario analysis was the best way to grapple with the many possible outcomes.

Working with both outside experts and with the client, we agreed on the key drivers that would shape the future. From those we developed a set of rational alternative scenarios for the market. We helped them narrow it down to three:

1. There will be a wave of consolidation as the incumbent players seek to build scale.

2. The new entrant's aggressive timetable would cause them to stumble and ultimately withdraw.

3. The customers would respond favorably or unfavorably to the entry of a powerful low-cost outside player with a less-than-spotless reputation.

Then we led a strategy war game for the client's senior leadership team. The scenario analysis helped them get past their lack of consensus, which was preventing them from dealing with the coming changes in their market. Armed with their Playbook, the now-aligned team had a clear set of tasks to work on, and a set of contingent strategies they had all agreed upon.

The most crucial part of the war game was what happened after it was over, when an aligned and confident team was able to take what they had practiced and execute it.

Competitive success does not stop at a war game, because the war game is basically just your locker room. You can't win the game unless you get out onto the field and put your strategies into play. Your Playbook, and what you do with it, is what differentiates your war game from an educational, interesting workshop to an actionable, winning competitive strategy.

REVISITING YOUR WINNING ASPIRATION

You might be wondering why I'm asking you what your winning aspiration is, when we just did that in chapter 6. This is because most companies, after doing a war game, realize that their winning aspiration has evolved.

At the beginning of this process, I asked you to think about what winning means to your company. You went through a war-gaming simulation to study the other players in the marketplace and how they're looking to win. Then you stress tested your strategies. Depending on how the game went, you may have gotten two different outcomes:

1. "What we had thought about initially still makes sense. Based on what we've seen in our war game will play out in the marketplace, we think we can be successful." With corporate confidence in your winning aspiration and strategies, you move forward.

2. "We took our winning aspiration into a war game and got decimated. The path that we were thinking about was based upon poor assumptions, blind spots and other factors." In your final round you would have revised your strategy. Here is also where you revisit your winning aspiration and make sure you've revised it in your Playbook.

Most people don't know that Microsoft used to have a cable set-top box business. Their strategy was, "We control computers and the operating systems for the computers. Why can't we control the operating system for set-top boxes?" They created a set-top box and tried to sell it to the major cable companies. Their winning aspiration was to be in every home in the US, but it wasn't happening.

We took them through a war game and the outcomes were not favorable. There was no path to success in a crowded market about to be disrupted with streaming and internet protocol boxes. They encountered blind spots like entrenched player relationships and consumer comfort with the user interface. Ultimately, they said, "Let's not waste our money. We're going to get out." They sold the business off after the game, saving billions of dollars and valuable time which enabled them to focus on other projects.

PICK AND CHOOSE YOUR BATTLES

If the war game answered for you the *So what?* then after your war game, you and your team will answer the *Now what?*

Picking and choosing your first real-world battles after you've war gamed helps you prioritize your opportunities and blind spots. Now you decide where you should focus in on first (e.g., low hanging fruit), for example, blind spots that you can easily fix with your current skill sets and other resources.

A large US retailer was looking to get into grocery, so they asked my company to run a war game for them. In the war game, the biggest blind spot they encountered was access to refrigeration. They used that to build their strategy, went straight to that blind spot after their war game, and now hold a double-digit share of grocery business in the US, making them one of the market leaders.

One pharmaceutical company with a new ophthalmology product we were war gaming realized very quickly that the opportunity in their market was significantly bigger than they had initially imagined it to be. They also saw that their competition was distracted with other initiatives. The company went straight into implementing their strategy with an aggressive direct-to-consumer ad campaign to capitalize on this fantastic opportunity and gained a huge competitive win in their market.

KEEP THE MOMENTUM GOING WITH NEXT STEPS

About three-to-six weeks after a war game, you will want to schedule your first touch point to go over the outputs of your Playbook, so that everyone does not just go back to their normal day-to-day jobs, forgetting all about the war game.

In your first touchpoint, you'll want to:

1. assign responsibilities, either to individuals or departments from your Playbook;

2. appoint a team to oversee the outputs from the Playbook (tech companies have entire teams responsible for competitors or competitive topics; these teams are responsible for ownership of competitive aspects moving forward); and

3. schedule progress reporting, or more touchpoints moving forward.

INTEGRATING YOUR WINNING STRATEGIES INTO YOUR BUSINESS

You'll also need to think about how war gaming will integrate into your core business activities. War gaming is not an isolated activity. Some companies integrate war gaming into their annual planning cycles. Others integrate it into strategy. Whichever you choose, you will want a regular cadence for war gaming and to calendar it, whether it's once a year, or multiple times a year. This ensures you get back into the real world and using the learnings from your Playbook, and that your employees share a common vocabulary to talk about competitive success.

TIMELINE FOR TAKING ACTION

Because your team has essentially practiced your strategy in the war game, none of this is coming out of left field for them. The momentum and internal alignment is already there, and can be translated into action immediately for the medium and long terms.

Think about your next steps in terms of a timeline. What do you need to do within the next few months then in six months, and then in a year from now?

Again, your key stakeholders in the company will be carrying out the actions that they already practiced in the war game. With a Playbook and a timeline, along with regular touchpoints along the way, everyone should be ready to execute winning strategies that will lead to competitive success.

MINI WAR GAMES

Once you've had experience with a large war game, you can easily have mini war games when a new strategy comes up due to changes in the marketplace. A mini war game is a quick scrimmage with one or two rounds incorporating scenarios. Of course, it's preferable to have comprehensive war games so that you get a 360-degree view of your market. But this way, you never enter into your market blindly, having tested your strategies to some degree before you implement them.

Refer to page 213 in the appendix for this chapter's template or scan the QR code in the appendix to download a full set of the printable digital templates for this book and bonus content containing an example of a Playbook.

CONCLUSION

I've been running corporate war games for twenty years for more than 200 diverse organizations worldwide. This includes advising sixty-eight of the top hundred companies in the Fortune Global 500 list and working with forty-one of the top fifty big pharma companies. I have also taught war games to students at Harvard (Cambridge, MA), MIT (Cambridge, MA), SMU (Dallas), IE (Madrid), ESMT (Berlin), IPADE (Mexico), and University of California (Irvine), and I never get tired of war gaming. Every war game reveals insights that nobody ever could have expected and, above all, is fun. In fact, I war gamed the idea for this book. And here we are.

Remember the Battle for Home Entertainment in 2006 that I told you about in chapter 7, when I was describing winning aspirations? I ended up running that same battle for my students again in 2022, adding Disney to the roster of teams. The winning aspiration was the same: Who is going to win the living room?

The students, you might recall, came up with the idea of Apple TV in 2006. This time they decided that the battle would be over content. Apple is being decimated by Netflix in terms of content, and for competitive success in this market, content is king. Disney is hurting, bringing back retired CEO Bob Iger. The Disney+ streaming service was a huge success during the pandemic, and, in fact, is the strongest asset in the Disney portfolio. All of this was in the Briefing Book. In the game, the Apple team made a move to acquire Disney. They had the resources to pull it off. Nobody saw that coming and the Apple team won the war game.

But this all happened in a classroom, right? A few weeks ago, I saw an article that announced[34] a rumor that Apple was aiming to acquire Disney. The rumors are flying, and leaders are scoffing. No way will the FTC allow it. I guess we will see....

I've described corporate war games and the different types you would use for your immediate needs, talked about how to prepare for a war game by creating your Briefing Book and Scenario Book and the logistics behind running a war game. I've also talked about creating your Playbook and how the most important thing is that you have a plan for using it, so that an interesting and fun corporate war game becomes actionable.

War gaming is an ongoing, lifelong process. For it to be successful, it can't just be a one-off. Integrate it into your company as part of your culture, with an open, humble, and curious mind, and you will build winning strategies that lead to competitive success.

I hope that some of these stories have helped you as you embark on your war-gaming adventure. Please feel free to reach out to me through my website www.CorporateWarGames.com or connect with me on LinkedIn if you have any questions and I'd be happy to share my resources and knowledge with you!

---

34 Kim Masters, "A Disney sale to Apple? Don't count it out this time," *The Hollywood Reporter*, August 11, 2023, https://www.hollywoodreporter.com/business/business-news/disney-apple-deal-1235559416/.

APPENDIX

S can the QR code below to download a full set of the printable digital templates for this book and bonus content containing an example of a Playbook and different war game structures.

CHAPTER 5

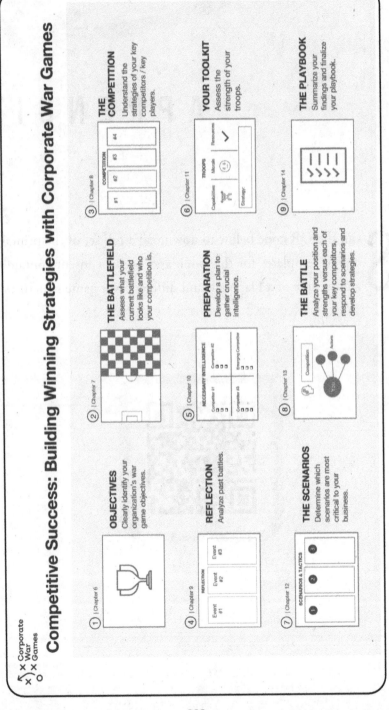

CHAPTER 6

X Corporate
X War
O X Games

(1)

Name: _____   Date: _____

WAR GAME OBJECTIVES
Chapter 6

Identify Your War Game Objective
What is your winning aspiration? Consider both short-term and long-term perspectives.

What game are you playing? How do you define your business? Describe what winning means to you.

What external assumptions do you want to pressure test? What external situations are you not prepared for? (competitors, suppliers, customers, regulatory environment, etc.)

What do you want to war game? Define your battle. Is it more important to prepare for a short-term or long-term battle?

CHAPTER 7

× Corporate
× War
× Games

(2)

Assess the Field of Battle
What does your competitive environment look like?

THE BATTLEFIELD
Chapter 7

Name: _____   Date: _____

DESCRIPTION OF THE BATTLEFIELD:
What does your competitive environment look like? What is at stake here? Is it crowded?

TIME FRAME:
What upcoming events/changes you need to prepare for? What are crucial dates to consider?

KEY CHANGES AFFECTING THE BATTLEFIED:
How quickly is it changing? What trends could affect your competitive environment? What are the key unknowns?

CHAPTER 8

$\begin{smallmatrix} x & \text{Corporate} \\ x & \text{War} \\ o & \text{Games} \end{smallmatrix}$ (3)

THE COMPETITION
Chapter 8

Identify the Enemy

Who are your key competitors / key players? Who are the emerging companies? What are their strategies? How will they compete against / with you?
Fill this template for each competitor / key player.

Name: _____   Date: _____

COMPETITOR / KEY PLAYER NAME:

Why is this company important?

What is their winning aspiration?

How can they attack or help you?

What is their intent and capabilities?

What is the level of threat? (critical, pesky, irritating, crucial, immanent, etc.)

What assumptions do they have?

CHAPTER 9

Name: _____   Date: _____

REFLECTION
Chapter 9

× Corporate
× War
× Games
(4)

Analyze Previous Battles

What significant events happened in the past? What challenged your organization? Analyze three past battles. Fill this template for each battles.

ANALYSIS:

What battle challenged the organization in the past?

Could this happen again? Why?

How has the organization changed in order to mitigate a similar battle?

What does the organization still need to change?

CHAPTER 10

x Corporate
x War
x Games
(5)

PREPARATION
Chapter 10

Name: _____

Date: _____

Gather Intelligence
What intelligence do you need in order to build your briefing book?

	Information Gaps/Intelligence Required	Source	Level of Importance	Owner
COMPETITOR #1				
COMPETITOR #2				
COMPETITOR #3				
EMERGING COMPETITOR				
OTHER				

x Corporate
x War
x Games

(6)

YOUR TOOLKIT
Chapter 11

Name: _____   Date: _____

Assess Troop Strength, Morale & Resources

What capabilities do you have in place to compete or differentiate? How is the morale? How strong are your resources? What needs to change?

WHAT DOES YOUR CURRENT TOOLKIT LOOK LIKE?

CAPABILITIES:

Weak   Medium   Strong

Strengths:

Weaknesses:

MORALE:

Poor   Fair   Great

Describe the Morale:

RESOURCES:

Lacking   Adequate   Strong

Key Resources:

Resource Gaps:

WHAT DOES YOUR FUTURE TOOLKIT NEED TO LOOK LIKE?

CAPABILITIES:

MORALE:

RESOURCES:

CHAPTER 12

x Corporate
x War
x Games

(7)

Name: _____

Date: _____

THE SCENARIOS
Chapter 12

Decide on Scenarios

What scenarios does your team need to keep top of mind?

QUICK PROCESS:

BRAINSTORM:

What are the scenarios (situations) that could affect your battlefield? (competitor enters, leaves, reduces pricing, litigation, mergers and acquisitions.)

DECIDE:

Narrow down your list to three scenario battles that your team needs to prepare for.

1
2
3

IN DEPTH PROCESS:

BRAINSTORM:

What are the key drivers that could affect your battlefield? Vote on top 2 super drivers. Define the extremes for each super driver (regulation, economic, social, technology, marketing mix etc.)

PLOT THE TWO SUPERDRIVERS; BUILD FOUR SCENARIOS:

Use the intersections of the two super drivers to determine your scenarios. Plot where the world is now and where it is moving towards.

Scenario 2

Scenario 1

Scenario 3

Scenario 4

1

2

x Corporate
x War
x Games

(8A)

Competitors Mindset

Think like your competitors. Be your competitors. Fill this template for each competitor to understand what they thinking and what moves they are likely to make.

THE BATTLE

Chapter 13

Name:

Date:

COMPETITOR NAME:

What is your winning aspiration? Where will you play?

What are your capabilities? What are your strengths/weaknesses?

What assumptions do you have? What do you believe about the market, competition, and your company?

How will you win?

What actions will you take?

Now-12 months

12 months+

x Corporate
War
x Games

(8B)

THE BATTLE
Chapter 13

Name: _____ Date: _____

Respond to Scenarios
How does this scenario change your thinking? How will you win in this situation?

Fill for each scenario.

SCENARIO:

What are the implications?

How do you think each competitor will react to the scenario?

What options do you have?

What actions will you take? How would you challenge the status quo?

Name: _____ Date: _____

X Corporate
X War
X Games (8C)

THE BATTLE
Chapter 13

The Competitive Battlefield

Fill this to analyze your position versus each of your key competitors and to formulate your competitive strategies in response.

COMPETITOR:				
What are your opportunities vs. competitor? What are your risks?				
What are your immediate actions/next steps?				
What offensive and defensive (proactive/reactive) actions can you take?				
What additional information is needed? What key competitive questions do you have for the future?				

$\times$ Corporate
$\times$ War
$\times$ Games

(9)

Summary

THE PLAYBOOK
Chapter 14

Name:

Date:

OBJECTIVE:
What does winning mean to your organization?

OPPORTUNITIES:
What are the most significant opportunities you have identified through this analysis?

ISSUES/BLIND SPOTS:
What are the most significant blind spots you have identified through this analysis?

ACTIONS:
What actions do you need to take now? 3-12 months? 12+ months? What do you need to stop doing?

| Now | 3-12 months | 12+ months |